D0108802

Pyotr Ilich Tchaikovsky

Play by Play

Pyotr Ilich Tchaikovsky | Play by Play

by
Alan Rich

with performances by
The Montréal Symphony
Orchestra
Charles Dutoit, conductor

A Newport Classic CD/B™
Presentation

HarperCollinsSanFrancisco,
1995

Credits

Executive Producer for the Series: *Lawrence J. Kraman*
Series Editor: *Jackson Braider*
Analytical Indexing: *John Ostendorf, Rudolph Palmer, Christopher Woltmann*
Art Director: *Ann E. Kook*
Interior Design: *Stuart L. Silberman*

This recording of *Symphony No. 5* was originally released on the London Label, #425 503-2. The *Romeo and Juliet Fantasy Overture* was released on the London label, #430 507-2.

Library of Congress Cataloging-in-Publication Data

Rich, Alan.
    Pyotr Ilich Tchaikovsky : play by play / by Alan Rich ; with
    performances by the Montréal Symphony Orchestra, Charles Dutoit conductor.
    p. cm.
    "A Newport Classic CD/B presentation."
    Discography: p.
    Includes bibliographical references (p.153).
    ISBN 0-06-263544-1   ISBN 0-06-263553-0
    1. Tchaikovsky, Peter Ilich, 1840-1893. 2. Tchaikovsky, Peter Ilich, 1840-1893.
    Symphonies, no. 5, op. 64 E minor. 3. Tchaikovsky, Peter Ilich, 1840-1893.
    Romeo et Juliette (Fantasy–Overture). 4. Symphonies—Analysis, Appreciation.
    5. Overtures—Analysis, Appreciation.

ML410.C4R52 1995 [B]   94-49111
780' .92—dc20   CIP
                                              MN

95 96 97 98 99 ❖ RRD(C) 10 9 8 7 6 5 4 3 2 1

Contents

A Note from the Executive Producer

IT IS NOT WITHOUT SOME IRONY that we have chosen to call the *Play by Play* series a "CD/B" presentation. Where the race is on in computer circles to define the *next* multimedia delivery system—though the various parties involved have never actually agreed as to what the current one is—we have concocted this marriage between two very different media, invented at least one millenium and half-a-world apart. It is, as you can see, very much a *low-tech* affair: a book and a compact disc.

Mind you, we have always been very conscious of the fact that this is a new medium. It isn't just a book with a CD pasted into it for fun, nor it is a CD with a hefty set of liner notes. Each illuminates the other; each brings something to the other what it might otherwise lack, particularly as regards the exploration, the appreciation, the *understanding* of music.

I feel a bit like Cecil B. DeMille in all of this: yes, the CD/B has been ten years in the making, but the cast has certainly not been in the thousands. Clayton Carlson and Bill Crowley, of HarperCollins and PolyGram respectively, caught on very quickly, and without their enthusiastic support, it is fair to say that none of this would have happened. The people in both their organizations—James McAndrew, Leslie Clagett, Justine Davis—have all been absolutely wonderful to work with.

Somewhere along the way, classical music became *serious* music, and when that happened, many of us lost touch with the idea that this music—heavy and heady as it can be sometimes—was very often supposed to be delightful, a pleasure, a source of enlightenment. I hope that this series will open up for you what has been, up to this point, a very closed world.

LAWRENCE J. KRAMAN

Author's Note

AS AN UNDERGRADUATE at Harvard, slogging my way through a pre-med major but with my heart in the Music Department, I learned to think about the listening experience as an ongoing narrative, full of thrills and surprises. The wonderful G. Wallace Woodworth would start a Haydn symphony on the 78-rpm record player, then pick up the tone arm and make us guess what was going to happen next. (We were usually wrong, but that wasn't the point.) I learned about the momentum of Beethoven's *Ninth Symphony* from Donald Tovey's measure-by-measure "précis" in the first volume of his *Essays in Musical Analysis* (omitted, for reasons not fathomable, in the current reprint edition of these essential musical insights). Woody in the classroom, and Tovey on paper, have shaped the way I think about listening to music over half a century. Now, however, I don't have to dash to the piano to play Tovey's musical squibs; I can hand them off, second-by-second or CD index-by-index, as clearly as if Woody were still up front running the Victrola. You can, too; that's what *Play by Play* will do for you, for me, and for music.

ALAN RICH
LOS ANGELES, 1995

How to Use This Book

THE CD included in this volume has been analytically indexed. That is to say, within each track on the compact disc there has been embedded a series of inaudible codes that allows the listener to access particular moments in the composition, be it something as quick as the entry of the bass part in a fugue or something as fundamental as the start of the recapitulation section in a sonata.

The various CD player manufacturers all have developed their own particular way of accessing the index points on a compact disc and the reader should consult his or her manual for the appropriate instructions. Some older models of machines have no such capacity. However, the trick in using the sections of this book devoted to Analytical Indexing—the *Play by Play* section and the *Essential Recordings* section immediately following it—is to look at the tracking display on the CD player and relate it to what you are reading about in the book.

Here is a typical example of how the code appears in the text: **[T2/i3, 1:29]**. This provides the reader three pieces of information: the track (**T2**), the index point (**i3**), and the absolute time of the event in the track (**1:29**). What this shorthand describes, then, is the third index point on the second track of the compact disc, which occurs at 1:29 into the track. So even if your CD player doesn't have indexing, the time display will give you a precise indication of the moment a particular event being described in the text occurs.

Tchaikovsky's Russia

INVASION AND RESISTANCE: these two events characterize much of Russia's history as far back as the days of the Mongol hordes. In 1812, Napoleon's battalions invaded Russia, confident of taking Moscow by Christmas, but they were turned back by the fierceness of the winter and the even fiercer tenacity of the Russian army. One-hundred-thirty years later, the same thing happened to the once-thought-invincible troops of Adolf Hitler's Germany.

What neither of those mighty armies could accomplish, musical forces from Western Europe had achieved most handily. Peter I (known as "the Great") was crowned Emperor of the Russias in 1721. At the time Russia was a nation culturally isolated from the rest of the world—be it European or Asian. Its only preserved music consisted of the body of chant jealously guarded by the monks of the Imperial Chapel. Counterpoint was introduced into this music only around

11

1680, mostly from the more developed musical societies in Poland and the Ukraine; the Old Believers in Moscow and St. Petersburg denounced this modernism as "Kievan part-singing." Around 1680, too, there came the first traces of a secular musical art, largely in the work of a Polish-trained Kievan, Nikolai Diletsky, who led a private choir in Moscow and developed a small school for hopeful composers. The military exploits of Peter the Great were celebrated by a series of secular cantatas, often with refrains where large choruses would sing something like "Vivat!" or "Hooray!" (The coronation scene in Mussorgsky's *Boris Godunov*, with its jubilant yells from the chorus, evokes the spirit of those earlier Russian pieces.)

Peter himself cared little for music, but he realized the ceremonial and psychological value of army bands. To that end, he brought in wind and brass players and drummers from Germany to form bands and also to teach music to Russians. Following Peter's death in 1725, and the death soon after of his son and successor, Peter II, his niece Anna was proclaimed Empress. Having little interest in running the government (a task she mostly relegated to her German lover, Ernst Johann Biron), Anna devoted her energies to building a cultural life for her Russians, where none had existed before. She hired Italian operatic troupes, who performed in newly built theaters in both Moscow and St. Petersburg. The first serious **opera** performed in Russia was Francesco Araja's *The Power of Love and Hate*, given in 1736 at the new St. Petersburg Imperial Theater. Its composer was the first of a long string of foreigners, mostly Italian, who ran that venue through the eighteenth century. By the 1780s, Italian opera had become a popular commodity in all of Russia's major cities. The day of the serious native Russian composer, however, had not yet dawned.

Catherine II (also "the Great") took the throne in 1764, and enhanced the steady diet of Italian opera with an admixture of the French styles. The Gallic comic operas were more to the taste of Catherine's French-speaking court, and they served as models for the first attempts by Russian composers to

Catherine II ("The Great"): Russia's enlightened Empress, who brought the European arts into her own country.

carve a niche for indigenous music: two one-act comic pieces performed in 1772, *Anyuta* and *The Wizard Lover*, by composers whose names have not survived.

The notion of a serious Russian musical repertory seems to have taken hold in the 1770s. A vogue for authentic Russian folk song developed, and a generation of composers was suddenly stirred to incorporate ancient homegrown melodies into operas, chamber works, even symphonies. Against the relative sophistication of the French and Italian imports this music is fairly feeble stuff, but it marks a beginning, at least, of the push to nurture a Russian repertory that would erupt into an obsession in the mid-nineteenth century.

Aside from the operas that flourished in the imperial theaters, most of the country's musical activity in the first decades of the nineteenth century was dominated by the aristocratic amateurs, some of them rich enough to maintain their own string quartets, orchestras, choruses, and opera companies. The first really important Russian composers mingled in these circles: Mikhail Glinka, who had studied in Italy and returned home eager to effect a union between the Italian *bel canto* style and Russian folk song; Aleksandr Dargomyzhky, whose fame abides in his opera *The Stone Guest*, another treatment of the Don Juan legend; and Aleksandr Alabyev, whose song "The Nightingale" still serves the needs of coloratura sopranos. An admitted amateur, Count Michal Wielhorski, composed symphonies, chamber works, and an opera, and was host in his St. Petersburg palace to Franz Liszt, Hector Berlioz, and the Schumanns. His father had been one of the founders of the St. Petersburg Philharmonic Society; Michal and his brother Mateusz helped establish a Concert Society "for the propagation of classical music in the best possible performances." In 1859 Mateusz sat on the board of the Imperial Russian Musical Society, which under the leadership of Anton Rubinstein would soon become the most potent force in revolutionizing and organizing Russia's music.

Until 1860, the best of Russia's musical life centered around St. Petersburg; Moscow's emergence as a musical hub would take place later on. St. Petersburg fairly teemed with music-making, as if to make up for the centuries when it had none. The Philharmonic Society, started in 1802, concentrated its efforts on large-scale choral works; its performers were mostly drawn from the ranks of the dilettantes, who ran the organization more for their own pleasure than the public good. The Society of Lovers of Music, founded in the 1840s, also admitted listeners only upon the recommendation of its members. Much livelier than either of these were the "Musical Exercises of the Imperial University," which assembled an orchestra of students (but not music students), ex-students, and outsiders to play new Russian works as well as the Viennese classics in ten yearly concerts open to the ticket-buying public—and filled the hall at every event. The "Exercises" were produced, however, without benefit of prior rehearsal, no doubt taking the Concert Society's dictum of "the best possible performance" to a dubious extreme.

The major controversy, which swirled for years and occupied Russian thought on all levels, was the debate between East and West: should Russian society expend its efforts in absorbing the influences and styles of Western Europe, or should those efforts go toward the development of an indigenous art? In 1804, Aleksandr I had ordained a public school system open to all comers, but obviously not to all doctrines. His education minister, Prince A. N. Golitzyn, encouraged university students to report professors or fellow students advocating any of the "dangerous, irreligious" ideas from the West. Even distinguished citizens outside academia—the poet Aleksandr Pushkin, for one—suffered harassment from the police for his political ideas; other writers, among them Nikolai Gogol and Mikhail Lermontov, were also carefully monitored by the agents of the bureaucracy. The journalist Pyotr Chaadayev, who in 1836 spoke out against Russia's cultural poverty as "a gap in the intellectual order" was declared mad by Tsar Nicholas I, confined to his house and forced to endure the humiliation of frequent psychological examinations.

Gradually, the borderlines between the two groups became somewhat blurred. The advocates of westernization (consider them liberals, using today's definition) and the Slavophiles (the conservative side, with strong support from the Russian Orthodox church) began to see some good in each other's doctrines. One major consideration that threatened the conservative point of view was the scope of Russia's land acquisitions under both Aleksandr and Nicholas, which brought into the Empire a host of varied cultures, from Georgia in the west to the Sakhalin Peninsula beyond Siberia. It was clearly impossible to impose a single outlook on life that could serve the needs of so widely diverse a territorial spread, with so many languages and so many religious sects.

Aleksandr Pushkin: Russia's first great poet and dramatist.

Mikhail Glinka (1804-57): Though trained in Italy, he returned to become Russia's first important composer.

The East-West controversy made itself known in all the arts, but in music most of all. Glinka's *A Life for the Tsar*, glorifying the heroism of a real-life character from Russian history, remained a tremendous success since its 1836 premiere. Despite its strong reflections of the *bel canto* ideals that Glinka had absorbed during his time in Italy, it stood out as a world-class piece of Russian operatic craftsmanship: the first opera on a Russian subject that dealt with peasants as well as nobles, and the first to include Russian folk tunes. Glinka's next opera, *Russlan and Ludmilla* (1842), was even more indigenous, less eclectically *bel canto*; it, however, was a failure. Its composer soon resumed his wanderings outside Russia, fell in love with Spain (as proven in his *Jota Aragonesa*) and died in Berlin in 1857, aged 53. He immediately became a hero back home. "Beethoven and Glinka!" Anton Rubinstein proclaimed, and probably even believed it.

The accession of Aleksandr II in 1855 represented a further strengthening force in Russian musical life. Rubinstein, as head of the

Imperial Russian Music Society, had the ear of the Grand Duchess Helena Pavlovna, the Tsar's aunt by marriage, and she came through with patronage and financial support. The Society was firmly in business, providing orchestral and chamber events on a higher level of

Criticism, Constructive and Destructive

Musical criticism, as a communicative bridge between practitioners of the art and prospective consumers, only came into its own early in the nineteenth century with the establishment in most major European cities of journals wholly devoted to music. Many leading composers wrote for these publications; Robert Schumann's essays, in his own *New Journal for Music,* aroused the world to the works of Chopin and Schubert. Criticism in the daily press came into its own later in the century, thanks above all to Vienna-based Eduard Hanslick, who for half a century (1855-1904) established standards not only for the music he most believed in but also for the responsibilities and qualifications for the practitioners of criticism. He did battle against Wagner, not because of his talent—he called him "the greatest living composer" early on—but because of the threat he posed to the traditions that music had clung to for centuries. His name lives on for the strength of his naysaying; Tchaikovsky seemed to be one of his pet anathemas. Witness his account that the Violin Concerto "stinks in the ear" and his absurd resistance to the 5/4 meter in the slow movement of the "Pathétique" Symphony, which he claimed would do just as well in the more common 6/8. But the eloquence and insight of his enthusiasms—for Verdi no less than Brahms—established his right to his opinions pro or con.

proficiency than St. Petersburg had hitherto enjoyed. A second society was inaugurated in Moscow in 1860, with Anton Rubinstein's brother Nikolay at the helm.

To some, however, the functions of the IRMS, and of Anton Rubinstein as a composer, signaled a sad comedown in the development of an authentic Russian art. The group variably known as "The Mighty Five," "The Russian Five", or, generically, "The Five"—militant advocates of a "Russian purity" in all the arts—believed the Rubinsteins and their schools represented the persistence of decadent, desiccated, Germanic influences. Mily Balakirev, the founder and acknowledged spokesman of the group, called the IRMS "a plot to bring all Russian music under the yoke of the German generals." To César Cui, another member, "it would be a serious error to consider [Anton] Rubinstein a Russian composer. He is merely [horror!] a Russian who composes." (Since Rubinstein is best known today for his sweet little salon piano piece, *Melody in F,* Cui may have had a point.)

Mily Balakirev had moved to St. Petersburg in 1855 from Nizhni Novgorod. His musical training had been spotty, but that didn't

Mily Balakirev (1837-1910): Largely self-taught as a composer and conductor, he became an influential figure in Russian music as the head of the composer group known as "The Five."

stop him from launching upon a career as composer. He was a man of strong opinions and a domineering personality, and soon after his arrival he succeeded in luring into his circle four other young countrymen, united in their determination to create an authentic Russian musical style, and also by the fact that none of them had had a formal musical education. Cui was a fortifications engineer by profession; Modest Mussorgsky, an eighteen-year-old ensign in the crack Preobrajensky Regiment with something of a drinking problem. Nicolay Rimsky-Korsakov was a naval officer who, also at eighteen, came to Balakirev practically on his knees, begging for composition lessons. Aleksandr Borodin, the last to join the group, was a chemist, whose teachers at medical school had scolded him for spending too much time at the piano.

Modest Mussorgsky (1839-1881): The most original of the Five, he drank himself to a premature oblivion and left a legacy of dazzling unfinished scores.

The Five met regularly with Balakirev, their self-appointed leader, studied scores of the classics, and helped each other with their own compositions. Each of them, Borodin wrote, "[was] made sincerely happy by the smallest success of another." The self-help continued even as the group dwindled;

Mussorgsky and Borodin died relatively young and, for better or for worse, Rimsky-Korsakov took on the task of editing some of their greatest scores—including Mussorgsky's stupendous *Boris Godunov* and Borodin's *Prince Igor*—into performable condition.

The pronouncements of the Five struck at the very basis of music: dramatic music must have an intrinsic worth; vocal music must agree with the sense of the words; orchestral music must honor Russia's own traditions; inspiration should be far more important than the rules of symphonic **form**. The academicians struck back, Tchaikovsky—newly graduated from the St. Petersburg Conservatory—among them. He found the Five's principles outrageous and self-indulgent. He pooh-poohed the idea of sitting around waiting for inspiration to strike. "[They] are very gifted persons," he wrote in 1878 in a famous letter to his patroness Nadezhda von Meck, "but they are all afflicted to the marrow with the worst sort of conceit and with a purely dilettantish confidence in their superiority over all the rest..."

Whatever the substance of these accusations and counter-accusations, they added to the liveliness of Russia's musical scene. The years from 1860 to 1900 witnessed a glorious outflowering of serious Russian music-making. Moscow emerged as a credible cultural rival to St. Petersburg; both cities boasted extensive and lavish state-run opera houses, Moscow's Bolshoi (founded in 1856) and St. Petersburg's Maryinsky (1860, later known as the Kirov), which in

1862 commissioned and produced the world premiere of Giuseppe Verdi's *La forza del destino.* Other cities, too—Tbilisi, in the newly-won state of Georgia, for one—developed strong resources. While the phenomenon of the amateur, self-taught composer had achieved some stability with the Five, the new conservatories in St. Petersburg and Moscow now began to turn out composers with more substantial training and a wider view of the musical world outside Russia, who in turn provided the growing Russian audience with a full and steady serving of music of all forms. Even Rimsky-Korsakov, in his early years an ardent advocate of Russian music and nothing but, accepted an academic post at the conservatory in St. Petersburg and filled his public concert programs with Bach, Handel, and Palestrina.

It was a golden era for Russian music, a propitious time to be born for a greatly talented musician. Pyotr Ilich Tchaikovsky was to discover that for himself.

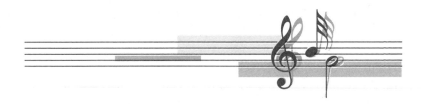

CHAPTER 2

The Early Years

THE TCHAIKOVSKY FAMILY was reasonably well-off. Ilya Petrovich Tchaikovsky was a mining engineer and manager of a foundry at Kamsko-Votkinsk, in the Vyatka province on the Volga River east of Moscow. Aleksandra Andreyevna, his second wife and mother of Pyotr Ilich—and of the older Ippolit and the younger Modest, Anatoly, and Aleksandra (Sasha for short)—was of French ancestry. Her father had been an epileptic, and she herself was of a nervous temperament. She can, therefore, be credited both with Pyotr's life-long attraction to French music and to that nation's culture overall as well as with the morbid sensitivity that would guide his pen and undermine his composure in the years to come.

There is no record of musical or literary talent among the Tchaikovsky ancestors, at least on the level that Pyotr and his ten-years-younger brother Modest would display. Pyotr (born 7 May

1840 in the reformed Russian calendar) seemed determined from an early age to make up for lost time. At four, he and his sister Sasha composed a song, "Our Mama in Petersburg" while Aleksandra was actually away on a visit to that city. A year later he began piano lessons with a local teacher, Mariya Palchikova, but soon surpassed everything she had to offer him. A prized family possession was an orchestrion, a descendant of the mechanical orchestra for which Beethoven had written his "Battle" Symphony (a clearly discernible ancestor of Tchaikovsky's own "1812" Overture) thirty years before. From the mechanized depths of that instrument, the young Tchaikovsky heard music by Bellini, Donizetti, Rossini and, more important, selections from Mozart's *Don Giovanni*, a work that remained close to him throughout his life. Another early influence on his musical explorations was a family governess, Fanny Dürbach, who taught him both French and German and helped him with some childish poetry, including a French poem about Joan of Arc.

In 1848 the family moved to St. Petersburg. Pyotr continued piano lessons, but these were curtailed when a severe attack of measles forced the child into six months of convalescence. A year later Ilya Petrovich took a new job out of town; his wife remained with Pyotr in St. Petersburg for a time, and he was enrolled in the preparatory classes for the School of Jurisprudence. Mother and son attended a performance of Glinka's *A Life for the Tsar*, still, after fourteen years, the most beloved of Russian operas; it made a lasting impression on the boy. Eventually his mother left him at the school and returned to her family; Tchaikovsky remembered the parting as "one of the most terrible days" of his life. The shock of that day remained with him, and was intensified by the death from scarlet fever of five-year-old Nikolai Modestovich Vakar, child of a close family friend. Tchaikovsky never got over the conviction that he had, somehow, brought the disease into the Vakar home. Other school friends remembered him as a moody child easily reduced to tears. "[Today] I celebrated my birthday and cried a lot," Pyotr wrote to his family in 1851, "but I had two friends with me, Belyavsky and Dokhturov, who comforted me." He continued, however, to mourn the separation from his parents, and his morose, whining letters eventually persuaded the family to move back to St. Petersburg.

In May 1852, Tchaikovsky passed his entrance examinations and enrolled in regular classes at the School of Jurisprudence. The family was reunited a few weeks later, adding to his joy. His brother Modest recalled how Pyotr would stand at the window of his dormitory room, blowing kisses to his mother. In Pyotr's own words, he loved his mother "with a kind of morbidly passionate love;" her sudden death from cholera in June 1854 was for him an unspeakable tragedy that cast a pall over the rest of his life. Twenty-five years after her passing, he confessed in a letter that "this was the first powerful grief I experienced...Every minute of that horrible day is etched on my memory as if it was yesterday."

One source of comfort the adolescent Tchaikovsky found just in time. He intensified his music studies, working simultaneously on singing and piano lessons and began to jot down musical ideas as they occurred to him. He considered an opera (based on Viktor Olkhovsky's *Hyperbole*), wrote a piano waltz, and in 1856 produced an insignificant trifle that would eventually become his first published work, a droopy Italian song called "Mezzanotte" ("Midnight"). Despite a few initial digressions, there was now no turning back from some kind of career in music. His piano teachers discouraged his ambitions toward becoming a piano virtuoso, but there were other possibilities for a life in music.

There was one other recourse, which would serve Tchaikovsky as a lifelong source of both consolation and torment—often simul-

St. Petersburg in the 1800s.

taneously. The School of Jurisprudence, like most men's institutions that nurture more intellectual pursuits, counted a considerable homosexual population among its students (and probably faculty as well). In his correspondence from his school years, including missives to his parents, Tchaikovsky chronicled his friendships with charming if ingenuous candor. One relationship stands out as particularly intimate, with the brilliant if erratic young poet Aleksey Apukhtin, and dates back to 1853. Mature and self-assured beyond his age, Apukhtin even at twelve had managed to charm practically the entire school, headmasters and students alike. He made no attempt to conceal his homosexuality, not from the world and certainly not from Tchaikovsky, his senior by a year. There is little doubt that Tchaikovsky had struggled with his "inclination" (his word in many letters) throughout his academic experience, and had poured a fair amount of clumsy passion into most of his friendships, fleeting or otherwise, at school. Even his taking up with Apukhtin provoked an outburst from Tchaikovsky's former, now deposed, "bosom friend."

The friendship with Apukhtin, which lasted the lifetimes of both men, firmed Tchaikovsky's grasp on his own inner torments. While their affair was not exclusive (beyond the first encounter, at least), Tchaikovsky drew some solace from being included in Apukhtin's circle of witty, creative, precocious ephebes. Though Modest Tchaikovsky describes him in his autobiography as "a pale, skinny little student whom I found displeasing but had to like because Pyotr liked him," Apukhtin was a born dominator, generous with his intimates but unbearably snotty to anyone else. To Tchaikovsky he composed poem after poem, love lyric after love lyric, and guided his friend's somewhat clumsier hand in creating verse of his own. Years later, several of Apukhtin's poems would turn up as texts to Tchaikovsky songs.

In 1859, Tchaikovsky completed his studies at law school and took a clerical position at the Ministry of Justice. He cut a dashing figure and moved freely through St. Petersburg society. In 1861, he traveled in western Europe, serving as interpreter for a friend of his father, and breathing for the first time the "forbidden" air of France, Germany, Belgium, and England. His father, meanwhile, had fallen on difficult times; an investment scheme had collapsed, leaving the family penniless and ending for the moment any hopes Tchaikovsky may have had of leaving his government post and becoming a professional musician. Nevertheless, he continued his studies in theory and composition at the institution founded by Anton Rubinstein, which by 1862 was officially known as the St. Petersburg Conservatory. Rubinstein offered considerable encouragement, and went about finding him piano and theory pupils, who arrived in sufficient numbers to finally enable Tchaikovsky to quit his job at the Ministry. Now—in 1863—and for the remainder of his life, he was fully, and for much of the time, contentedly, engaged in music.

Tchaikovsky remained at the Conservatory another two and a half years, studying flute and organ as well as composition. In 1865, his father remarried; that summer Pyotr and his two younger brothers joined him at the home of Lev Davïdov, their brother-in-law, near Kiev. Tchaikovsky had hoped to spend time exploring the folk songs of that region, but found that most of the peasants had already become so Westernized that their music was corrupted; he did work one song, however, into a string quartet **movement** and a scherzo for piano. In the town of Pavlovsk that September, the visiting Johann Strauss, Jr. conducted a set of dances that Tchaikovsky had composed earlier in the year. In November, Tchaikovsky made his first foray onto a podium, conducting the student orchestra in his *Overture in F*. One work from Tchaikovsky's student days even achieved some circulation, an overture for Aleksandr Ostrovsky's play *The Storm*. Tchaikovsky had toyed with the idea of setting the entire play as an opera (as Leos Janácek was to do, seventy years later, as *Katya Kabanova*); restraint, however, prevailed. The piece is full of a young man's brilliance: a little Berlioz, a lot of Liszt, a Russian folk song to establish legitimacy. Rubinstein disliked the work, and lavished further scorn on a cantata based on Schiller's "Ode to Joy" which Tchaikovsky presented as his graduation piece (for which he earned a silver medal). That piece also drew down the public wrath of César Cui, critic and member of the Five. The young composer, in other words, had arrived.

CHAPTER 3

Pyotr Hits His Stride

IN SEPTEMBER 1865, Nikolay Rubinstein approached Tchaikovsky with a job offer: to come to Moscow after his graduation from the St. Petersburg Conservatory to be harmony professor at Nikolay's school, the Moscow branch of the Russian Music Society, which Anton Rubinstein had established with his brother as director. The Moscow campus was flourishing; in 1866 it assumed the more glorious title the Moscow Conservatory.

Tchaikovsky arrived in the city in January 1866, and Nikolay took him into his own home. Unlike the more conservative Anton, Nikolay was friendly toward the younger, innovative talents among Russian composers, even the members of the Five. The new post did not pay well, but it did, at least, leave Tchaikovsky time to compose. In March, Nikolay conducted the school orchestra in a revised version of Tchaikovsky's schoolboy work, the *Overture in F,* and also persuaded his young colleague to consider embarking on writing a symphony.

No previous composition had cost Tchaikovsky as much, in both mental and physical effort, as this *First Symphony.* It was fully sketched by June, but the orchestration caused him great agony. He took the work, which he had titled *Winter Dreams,* back to St. Petersburg to show to Anton Rubinstein, who censured it vehemently. Tchaikovsky returned to Moscow to revise it. Nikolay Rubinstein conducted one movement, the scherzo, in Moscow in December; it was coolly received. The entire symphony was performed in St. Petersburg in February 1868; this time the reception was generally favorable. The work's mingling of charm and a certain amount of likable, youthful clumsiness won it a place in the repertory for a time. It is still performed, largely on the strength of the composer's name it bears. Tchaikovsky worked feverishly, struggling to make his mark over a wide swath in Moscow circles. He determined to fashion an opera on Ostrovsky's *The Voyevoda,* and persuaded the playwright to provide a libretto. Tchaikovsky then proceeded to lose Ostrovsky's manuscript, and ended up writing most of the text himself. In any case, the work was poorly met, lasting only five performances. Tchaikovsky later destroyed the score, but cannibalized some of the material into his later opera, *The Oprichnik.* (A much later **tone poem** bears the same name as *The Voyevoda,* but none of its music.) Undaunted, he completed another opera, based on the Ondine legend; this one never reached the stage, although again Tchaikovsky found other uses for some of its music.

Life in Moscow had its lighter side as well. In the summer of 1867, Pyotr and his brother Modest spent six weeks at the country home of their sister Aleksandra, who apparently entertained hopes of pairing her brothers off with her two sisters-in-law Vera and Elizaveta Davïdova; nothing eventuated beyond routine cordiality. A year later, however, Pyotr experienced his first, however brief, awakening of interest in the opposite sex. In September 1867 he made the acquaintance of the singer Désirée Artôt, and furnished her with some extra music for an opera (not his) in which she was appearing. The two spent considerable time together, and Pyotr wrote to his father and to Désirée's mother stating they wished to be married. Both parents, along with Tchaikovsky's closest friends, opposed the match. In any case, Désirée settled the problem herself by marrying a Spanish singer. For the next decade, Tchaikovsky seems to have had no further involvement with women.

In other regards, Tchaikovsky moved easily in Moscow's culture-conscious society. Nikolay Rubinstein went out of his way to cater to Tchaikovsky's needs and to present him in his own musical world, with mixed results. "When he has been drinking," Tchaikovsky wrote of his benevolent host, "he likes to say that he has a tender passion for me, but when he is sober he can annoy me to the point of tears." Hector Berlioz visited Moscow in December 1867, and

Tchaikovsky served as the visitor's guide, delivering a handsome eulogy in French at a ceremonial banquet.

The formidable Balakirev had also come to Moscow to attend Berlioz' concerts, and he and Tchaikovsky hit it off reasonably well; Tchaikovsky later journeyed to St. Petersburg and was cordially received by the rest of Balakirev's coterie. He dedicated a symphonic poem called *Fatum* to Balakirev, who conducted it in March 1869—and then launched into a diatribe against the piece. In true Tchaikovskian fashion, Tchaikovsky expunged the score, while leaving enough orchestral parts in circulation that the work could be reconstructed, as it was three years after Tchaikovsky's death. Tchaikovsky was stung by Balakirev's criticisms, but bent over backward to remain on friendly terms.

That effort paid off. Balakirev suggested to Tchaikovsky that he consider a piece drawn from Shakespeare, and proffered an outline for a tone poem on the subject of Romeo and Juliet. The suggestion struck gold: in March 1870, Nikolay Rubinstein conducted the first version of what, after considerable revisions, would stand forth as Tchaikovsky's first masterpiece. Although it would be another sixteen

Nikolay Rubinstein (1835-1881): Younger brother of Anton, founder of the Moscow Conservatory, wise supporter and bitter critic of Tchaikovsky's music.

years before the *Romeo and Juliet Fantasy-Overture,* as Tchaikovsky called it, would reach the public in its final state (completed in 1880, it was first performed in Tbilisi in 1886), it had already done much to boost its composer's self-esteem and enjoyed particular success among the intimates who had watched the score take shape.

Even so, his compositions in the early 1870s showed a curious dichotomy. On the one hand, there were works of truly epic character, mingling Tchaikovsky's genuine passion for Russian folk tunes with the grasp of European structural techniques and orchestration

Romeo and Juliet in Music

Well over thirty entries appear under "Romeo and Juliet" in the *Concise Oxford Dictionary of Opera;* to these we can add the non-operatic treatments such as Hector Berlioz' *Roméo et Juliette* dramatic symphony, Tchaikovsky's *Fantasy-Overture,* sets of incidental music for the play by David Diamond and others, and Sergey Prokofiev's sublime ballet score. Don't leave out the Leonard Bernstein/Stephen Sondheim *West Side Story* or the less-known (but delightful)

"Romanoff and Juliet" by Peter Ustinov. Leave room in your affections, too, for Judy Holliday's immortal line in *Bells Are Ringing,* proving that if Romeo and Juliet had had access to a telephone-answering service, "Those two kids would be alive today!"

Among the operatic versions, several play fast and loose with Shakespeare's text. Georg Benda's 1776 opera begins with the couple already married and moves on to a happy ending, with Juliet awakening in her tomb before Romeo can stab himself. Charles-François Gounod's opera sweetens the story that his contemporaries among the Five so totally deplored. In April 1872, he completed *The Oprichnik*, his first truly successful opera. (It, too, narrowly escaped destruction by the distraught composer. Fortunately, this time a copy of the score was already in a publisher's hands.) The work, dealing with love and conspiracy among the oprichniks, the legendary bodyguards of Ivan the Terrible, was successful at the time, although it has now fairly well vanished from the repertory. The *Second Symphony*, begun in June, enjoyed a more lasting success—again, however, only after painful revamping. After

with a wedding scene and a ballet, and ends up more Gounod than Shakespeare. Vincenzo Bellini's *I Capuletti ed I Montecchi* ("The Capulets and the Montagues") also strays some distance from the Bard, but at least honors the play's tragic ending. So does Frederick Delius' *A Village Romeo and Juliet,* set in a mystical place where a character named the Dark Fiddler lures two young lovers into his boat, which sails downstream and eventually into another world.

It's easy to understand why the drama has lent itself to musical treatment so often; the dualism between the warring families and the lovers themselves suggests a lyrical form in itself, which the twenty minutes of Tchaikovsky's orchestral distillation captures almost as well as the three hours of Shakespeare's play. He never went so far as to envision an opera about the star-crossed lovers, but did sketch a love duet, using, of course, the love themes from the orchestral work; it was found in his papers after his death, and completed by the Russian composer Sergey Taneyev.

Tchaikovsky's death, the work became known as *Little Russian* and it does, indeed, incorporate a number of folk melodies and, in the last movement, a whirling dance tune worthy of Mussorgsky. (It also comes to a climax on a single resounding note on the gong, an effect Tchaikovsky again used, in a far different mood, in the last movement of his *Pathétique Symphony* twenty-one years later.)

On the other hand, in those years Tchaikovsky was also drawn to the production of a gentler and even trivial kind of music: a set of rather sentimental, salon-style songs (of which one, based on a Goethe poem but universally known as "None But the Lonely Heart,"

Tchaikovsky's Cameo Appearances on Your Hit Parade

Nobody knows for sure when the practice of turning the melodies of Tchaikovsky (and Chopin and Rachmaninoff) into pop ballads and dance numbers began. The process was gradual; after all, the most successful sentimental songwriters in the big band era had probably soaked up a lot of Tchaikovsky subliminally, and put it to good use. As early as 1935 Glenn Miller had worked the Love theme from *Romeo and Juliet* into something called "A Blues Rhapsody"; the more familiar version (a song called "Our Love") came out four or five years later. The bandleader Freddy Martin played a major role in getting Tchaikovsky onto the charts in 1938, with "Tonight We Love," a direct steal from the start of the *First Piano Concerto*. Soon after, Mack David and André Kostelanetz produced their "Moon Love," based on the horn solo in the *Fifth Symphony*. Buyers of complete recordings of the *First Piano* enjoys a certain fame); and a rather tame string quartet (again, with one tune destined for popularity, a refrain in the slow movement that later made it to Tin Pan Alley under the title "The Isle of May"). A second quartet, composed in 1874, maintained the conventional manner. Tchaikovsky noted that the piece had taken less work than anything he had previously written, and that may, in fact, be mirrored in the music's bland unfolding.

It was at this time, furthermore, that Tchaikovsky extended his activities in yet another direction. In 1871, he became the music critic of the Moscow publication *Contemporary Chronicle;* the job provided

Concerto and the *Fifth Symphony* are often startled to discover that the works contain a lot more than their respective come-on tunes—as is also the case, by the way, with Richard Strauss' *Also Sprach Zarathustra.*

But the grandest of all reworkings is the final scene of *Tsaritza,* the fictitious opera ("by the great Trentini") that enlists the fortissimo services of Jeanette MacDonald and Nelson Eddy at the end of *Maytime,* a splendid example of romantic cinematic slush from 1937. The music is all from

the *Fifth Symphony:* a monk's chorus, complete with deep, deep bassos, takes on the opening Fate theme; that theme, in its triumphant final form, resounds in some kind of patriotic pageant. At the end Jeanette, newly-crowned Empress of all the Russias, bids farewell to her traitorous lover Nelson to the "love theme" (aka "Moon Love") from the second movement, as he is marched off to face the firing squad.

Ah, they don't make 'em like that anymore.

a smattering of extra income and, more importantly, kept Tchaikovsky in close touch with the swirl of musical life in the capital. He argued brilliantly in his allotted space, deploring the Russian taste that cultivated the banalities of Italian opera and ignored the strength of native music, and attacked with equal fervor the corruption of Russian folk heritage at the hands of composers bent on turning noble melodies into salon tunes. He refused to accept the Slavophile point

Tchaikovsky portrait: Looking very professorial, from the early 1870s.

of view, that every musical idea from Western Europe incorporated into Russian music constituted an anathema; his writing, as his music, sought out some kind of balance. For this, however, he was widely assailed; supporters of Russian "purity" mingled personal innuendo into their protests on musical grounds. After four years of both hurling and enduring slings and arrows, Tchaikovsky ceased his critical activities. Yet his collected letters, no less than his published articles, reveal the workings of a sharp and perceptive mind.

One more work, an opera titled *Vakula the Smith*, culminated the part of Tchaikovsky's creative life in which allegiance to his Russian heritage played the major role. The text came from Gogol's comedy *Christmas Eve*, a splendid satirical fantasy whose characters include the Devil, along with the lovers Vakula and Oxane. Almost all the music bears a Russian stamp, much of it an unconscious but direct tribute to the ancestor of native opera, Mikhail Glinka, whose music Tchaikovsky had long adored. *Vakula* remained among Tchaikovsky's favorite scores—a feeling not, however, shared at the December 1876 premiere. As usual, Tchaikovsky later refurbished the work; in its later form, known variously as *The Slippers* and *Les caprices d'Oxane*, the opera still awaits a proper revival.

Vakula can be said to mark the end of Tchaikovsky's "high nationalistic" period, although his style never completely forswore the colorations of indigenous Russian music. What replaced it was a more personal manner of composition, given sometimes to outcries of deep tragedy, even morbidity, certainly more emotionally involving—but at the same time reflecting a growing allegiance to the expressive devices of Western European music. Robert Schumann's music, with its robust momentum of harmonic language, the striving for structural unity within the large outlines of a four-movement symphony of chamber work, was an especially strong influence, for better or worse. The "worse" side showed itself in Tchaikovsky's *Third Symphony*, begun in 1875. Clearly beholden to the shape of the Schumann "Rhenish" Symphony, the Tchaikovsky score absorbed Schumann's charm, but also his long-windedness. The *Third Symphony* (sometimes known as the *Polish*) is not one of Tchaikovsky's most distinguished scores.

In August 1875, Tchaikovsky began work on his first ballet, a commission from Moscow's Imperial Theater, whose lavish, evening-long dance creations enjoyed a passionate following. Starting with some small dance pieces he had earlier composed for his sister Aleksandra's children, Tchaikovsky created a balletic masterpiece, *Swan Lake*, that, even on its own, comes together with musical logic and strength unknown in the pallid dance pieces that theaters had hitherto subsisted upon.

The year 1875 also marked the *First Piano Concerto*, Tchaikovsky's debut in that musical form. Its history is familiar lore: Nikolay Rubinstein angrily rejecting the dedication and pronouncing the work unplayable, a substituted dedication to Hans von Bülow, and that German virtuoso performing the work's world premiere in, of all places, Boston, in October. "Striking, brilliant but sometimes bizarre," were some of the adjectives the formidable John Sullivan Dwight applied to this "difficult, strange, wild, ultra-modern Russian **concerto**…But could we ever learn to love such music?" History has furnished the answer.

Hans von Bülow (1830-1894): To the eminent German pianist and conductor fell the premiere of Tchaikovsky's Piano Concerto No. 1—*in Boston!*

Tchaikovsky's Women

THE ROMANCE BETWEEN TCHAIKOVSKY and the opera singer Désirée Artôt lasted a mere six months. Tchaikovsky first met her when she visited Moscow in early 1868. He became infatuated with her, but did nothing to press himself upon her until September of that year, when she returned to appear in Daniel François Auber's *Le domino noir*, for which he composed a few extra numbers. For a while she seems to have returned the compliment of Tchaikovsky's attentions; by late fall, as Anatoly Tchaikovsky noted in a letter to his brother, "in Moscow all anyone talks about is your marriage to Artôt." And, as Pyotr wrote to Anatoly's twin Modest, he had been devoting all his spare time to "the one person, of whom you have no doubt heard, whom I love very, very much."

Désirée was five years Tchaikovsky's senior, a fact that caused concern to both his and her friends, and there is justifiable cause to wonder how seriously she took the composer's courtship. One observer described her as a "thirty-year-old spinster...who is just beginning to grow stout," and we can guess that Tchaikovsky was enamored more with her artistry than her personal allure. In any case, she had no intention of abandoning her operatic career, which was mostly based in Paris and included a large circle of admirers. One of these, a wealthy Armenian whom Moscow society knew only as "X," sat in the front row at all her performances and showered her with gifts. If her union with Tchaikovsky had been subjected to a vote among both Désirée's family and Tchaikovsky's social contacts, it would have been defeated almost unanimously.

Fortunately, it never came to that. In February 1869, Nikolay Rubinstein, who had expressed great fears about his protégé's defection from Moscow's cultural scene into the arms of Désirée, jubilantly informed Tchaikovsky that his beloved had herself defected into a marriage with one Mariano Padilla y Ramos, a Spanish baritone from her own opera company. Delight reigned supreme in Tchaikovsky's clan. "Mme. Artôt's action pleases me," his father wrote.

It was not quite the end of the Désirée chapter, though. She sang in St. Petersburg in October 1869, and this time it was Modest who was driven to "indescribable ecstasy," as he put it in a note to Pyotr. The lady and the Tchaikovskys didn't cross paths for another six years. She and Pyotr met again in December 1875, when they did little more than glare at one another. "She has grown fat to the point of ugliness," the disenchanted Pyotr wrote to his brother Anatoly, "and has nearly lost her voice."

By then Tchaikovsky had regained his position as the darling of Moscow's cultural crowd. He had moved out of Nikolay Rubinstein's house in 1871 into lodgings of his own. Anecdotes abound of his showing up at masked balls in women's costumes and of the various young men who gained his amorous attentions. One of these was Eduard Zak, who first caught Tchaikovsky's eye in 1869 as a fifteen-year-old Moscow Conservatory student—the peak age, the composer mused, "for the tenderness and sweetness of love." Tchaikovsky took the lad into his home, bestowing him with both affection and protection. Then, at nineteen, Eduard committed suicide. The tragedy shook Tchaikovsky deeply; fourteen years later, he would write in his diary that he still "thought much and long of Eduard. Wept much." His one true soul mate during those years was his brother Modest, with whom he willingly shared his most intimate thoughts—and, occasionally, certain of his lovers as well. Immersed as he was in Moscow's widespread homosexual society, with its hordes of truly brilliant creators but also its subcultures who lived mostly for visits to the city's male prostitute underground, he realized the futility of hiding his "affliction." It was, of course, a society living at a volcano's edge; Russian law stipulated severe penalties against such proclivities. Gossip and blackmail were rife; they added to Tchaikovsky's long-standing fear of crowds and public acclaim. "I am a person," he wrote, "who has a supreme and insurmountable aversion for publicity in general and newspaper publicity in particular. For me there is nothing more terrible...than to be the object of public attention."

If Tchaikovsky could manage, to some degree, to avert his face from public scrutiny, he could not divert the actions of private individuals. As it happened, the years 1876-77 brought two women into his life whose impact was far stronger than any previous relationship: the patroness Nadezhda Filaretovna von Meck, whom he never actually met; and the passionate groupie Antonina Milyukova, whom he never *should* have met.

Nadezhda Filaretovna Frolovskaya was the daughter of a music lover and landowner. At sixteen she married Karl von Meck, a German engineer who amassed a considerable fortune, and died in 1876, leaving his widow well-off, but with eleven children. Nine years older than Tchaikovsky, she was a woman of formidable intellect, well-read and sensitive to the latest developments in all the arts. The staff at her Moscow estate included resident musicians; in later years the young Claude Debussy was to become a live-in tutor for her children. In 1876, her artist-in-residence happened to be the violinist Josif Kotek, Tchaikovsky's friend and former pupil. It was Kotek who first made his employer aware of Tchaikovsky's music, along with the information that the composer could use some financial aid. She immediately commissioned Tchaikovsky to create violin versions of some of his small early pieces, and a funeral march to serve as memorial for her late husband. In this negotiation, Kotek served as go-between.

In March 1877, there began a correspondence between Tchaikovsky and his new patroness, of an extent and self-revelation seldom matched in literary history. Still mourning the death of her husband of twenty-nine years, von Meck withdrew into total seclusion, even to the point of avoiding contact with her children's in-laws. Imperious by nature, she bullied her staff and demanded strict control over their private lives. "I am very unsympathetic in my personal relationships," she wrote on 3 March 1877, in one of her first letters to Tchaikovsky, "because I do not possess any femininity whatever...I do not know how to be tender." She could have been, one might think, the ideal close companion for the misogynistic Tchaikovsky.

She had paid Tchaikovsky handsomely—excessively so, even in his eyes—for the first sheaf of commissioned works. Now, only two months after the start of their "relationship," he was emboldened to request a loan of 3,000 rubles. She responded by proposing twice that sum—6,000 rubles, approximately $3500 in American money at the time—as a yearly stipend, to maintain his freedom to compose. "As for the means of repayment," she wrote, "I ask you, Pyotr Ilich, not to think of this or to trouble yourself." There was, however, one provision: they were never to meet.

Reading the fourteen years' worth of correspondence between Nadezhda von Meck and her "beloved friend," one is struck over and again by seeming contradictions. On one hand she demanded isolation from personal contact; on the other, she seemed anxious to drink in the whole of him. "I am so interested in knowing everything about you," she wrote in that same early letter, "that at almost any time I can say where you are and...what you are doing. From everything I myself have observed in you and have heard...I have conceived the most cordial, kindly and enthusiastic feelings for you." Over the years, she begged him for photographs, and at one point requested that he walk past her home at a given time, so that she could observe him from afar.

At first Tchaikovsky begged for a meeting; soon, however, he developed his own elaborate rationale why this should not happen. "It does not surprise me in the least that, having come to love my music you do not seek an acquaintance with its author. You are afraid not to find in me those qualities which your idealizingly inclined imagination has attributed to me..." Nadezhda disagreed, however; she was already convinced, she insisted, that Tchaikovsky possessed all the attributes of her ideal. "I fear acquaintance with you for quite a different reason..." What that might have been, she left no clue; perhaps her age and unprepossessing appearance had something to do with it, perhaps not. In any case, her "beloved friend" had his hands full with another woman who had suddenly come into his line of sight.

In April 1877, the composer received an ardent love letter from a certain Antonina Milyukova, who claimed that they had met at the Conservatory (which Tchaikovsky could not remember) and that her adoration for his music had drawn her to adore its creator as well. Further letters followed; she would kill herself, she pledged, if he spurned her. Tchaikovsky visited her in June, and gently informed her that he could not love her.

There the matter might have rested except for one thing. Aleksandr Pushkin's great lyric poem "Eugene Onegin" had been brought to his attention, and he had already begun work on an operatic version. He was, in fact, immersed in the crucial scene, Onegin's rejection of Tatyana's passionate letter with its declaration of love, when Antonina arrived on the scene. When Tchaikovsky recognized the parallel between her situation and that of Tatyana, he returned to Antonina and proposed marriage—on the condition that physical consummation would not take place. They were married on 18 July.

Disaster struck almost immediately (although not with the force depicted in Ken Russell's film, *The Music Lovers*, a rather free biographical treatment to say the least). Terrified by the new entanglement, Tchaikovsky left home on the pretext of taking a cure in the Caucasus, fleeing instead to his sister Aleksandra's country home, which had served as refuge often in the past, where he remained until the start of the new term at the Conservatory mandated his return to Moscow and to Antonina. His desperation now renewed—Antonina was now demanding that he sleep with her—he attempted a clumsy suicide in the Moscow River (either by drowning or by catching a chill), was rescued and achieved a second escape—this time to Switzerland. There a doctor presented him with the welcome news that he must never return to Antonina.

Their separation was not pleasant. By the start of 1878, Tchaikovsky and Antonina had begun divorce proceedings. He sent her whatever small amount of money he could; the pension from

Nadezhda had not yet begun. Antonina, meanwhile, had turned vengeful, dashing off letters to Tchaikovsky's father, his publisher, and some of his friends exposing her husband's monstrous behavior. Modest hired a private detective to prove Antonina an adulteress. Through her outside interests, she produced three children in the years following the divorce.

In 1886, some irrational impulse drove her once again to seek a reconciliation with Tchaikovsky, asking him to take her children (one

Fact and Fantasy

Ken Russell's *The Music Lovers* is to the facts of Tchaikovsky's life what a large and bouncy St. Bernard named Beethoven is to that composer: a total fabrication, irresistible in its own fantasy world. To wit: in the film, Tchaikovsky as a small boy is psychologically deeply wounded by the spectacle of his cholera-infected mother soaking in a therapeutic hot bath. (He was actually fourteen.) Antonina Tchaikovsky, shortly after her marriage to Pyotr, is tortured by madmen in an asylum. (In fact, she wasn't committed until three years after her husband's death.) Nadezhda von Meck is seen turning Tchaikovsky away when she learns of his homosexuality (despite the prevalence of that "affliction" among her own in-house musicians), so that he must then become a conductor to support himself. (He had begun conducting nearly twenty years before Nadezhda came into his life, and wrote her often about his experiences on podiums throughout Europe.)

Moral: Movies that tell the truth about a composer's life are likely to be as dull as movies about bricklaying.

of which she had named Pyotr) and requesting that he dedicate some small piece of work to her. Even nine years after their separation, the letter sent him into a hysterical rage, punctuated—so he claimed—with an attack of hemorrhoids. By then, however, Tchaikovsky could afford to settle a fair sum on Antonina. Three years after Tchaikovsky's death, she was committed to an insane asylum, where she spent her last twenty years. Modest visited her regularly.

Nadezhda von Meck, to her everlasting credit, took the episode of Tchaikovsky's marriage with wise forbearance; very likely she had sensed its implications and dangers from afar better than its participants did at close range. "I am sure, my dear good friend," she wrote shortly before the wedding, "that neither in your new or in any position will you forget that you...will see in me only a person who is close to you and loves you..."

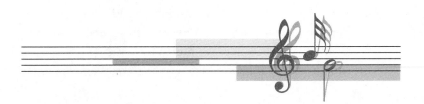

Mastery in Eclipse

IN JANUARY 1878, Tchaikovsky completed the scoring of his *Fourth Symphony,* and, a month later, *Eugene Onegin.* The former work was dedicated to Nadezhda von Meck; both she and Tchaikovsky continually referred to it in their correspondence as "our" symphony. It had its first performance on 22 February and was quite happily received by the Moscow audience. The troubles with Antonina had not yet slowed his pen; he had done most of the work on both the new symphony and the opera during his first flight from the marital bed the summer before.

Nadezhda teased him to compose a "program" for the symphony. The peremptory, brassy summons that begins the work, interrupts the course of the first movement several times, and returns just before the end of the fourth movement he described as a "Fate" motive—as he would describe several themes in other works over the rest of his life. The new symphony represented something of an advance in Tchaikovsky's mastery of symphonic structure. Its first and last movements show a kind of rude energy, under better control than, say, the battle music in *Romeo and Juliet*; the finale uses a folk tune turned by rhythmic quirks into a drunken dance. The many shifts of **tonality** within each movement, sudden shifts from one key to another key quite remotely related, indicate an arrogant disregard for the old-fashioned **classical** rules; here was a composer very much the master of his own musical voice. The melancholy slow movement and the deliciously scored scherzo—nothing but pizzicato strings at first and at the end, and a ballet-like middle section for winds—are a welcome relief from the violence; overall, the work represented a major forward step for Tchaikovsky in managing large-scale symphonic structures.

Onegin was first performed in March 1879, in a rather shaky production by students at the Moscow Conservatory; it would be a while, therefore, before it achieved its deserved acclaim. Beyond question the finest of Tchaikovsky's operas, it was in many ways his finest music to date in any form. Undoubtedly his early regard for Antonina went into the music for the opera's heroine—the fragile, vulnerable Tatyana, enamored of the dashing but caddish Onegin, rudely cast aside, grown later into a strong and desirable woman who can then return the insult. The sweep of the opera's music, from the balletic elegance of the party scenes to the anguish of the protagonists, gave the lie to any notion that the crisis in Tchaikovsky's personal life had yet in any way affected his work.

That eventuality, however, came to pass soon enough. Even before the Antonina episode, a kind of hysteria had sporadically entered into Tchaikovsky's compositions. The *Fourth Symphony* was laid out on a plan sufficiently spacious to allow its musical heat room to circulate. The tone poem "Francesca da Rimini," composed just before the symphony, was not so fortunate; its tense outcries in the telling of misbegotten love and betrayal seemed too heavily beset by the winds of Dante's Inferno for its allotted twenty-or-so-minute extent. ("An ear-flaying horror," reported a Berlin critic on the work's

Fate's Fickle Finger

"So knocks Fate at the door..." These words, attributed to Beethoven as the explanation to his student Ferdinand Ries of the rhythmic figure that dominates the *Fifth Symphony* (but just as likely coming from Ries' own imagination), began one of music's great ongoing pieces of gadgetry. Here, for the first time, was a symphony unified by a recurrent musical figure—and what's more, a figure

with a Romantic title attached. Giuseppe Verdi designed a striding Fate motive to tie together his otherwise sprawling opera *La forza del destino*, where it occurs every time the avenging baritone overtakes the fleeing soprano. (The opera had its world premiere in St. Petersburg in 1862, where Tchaikovsky surely saw it.) A similarly arresting Fate motif shows up in Bizet's *Carmen* every time the lady's charms ensnare the hapless tenor. Franz Liszt identified his tone poem *Les Préludes* as the account of Man's

first performance there.) More heartache accompanied the *Violin Concerto*, completed later in 1878—inspired by the same Josif Kotek who had engineered Tchaikovsky's alliance with Nadezhda von Meck but dedicated to the eminent virtuoso Leopold Auer. It was rejected by Auer as "unplayable" and was badly received at its first performance (in Vienna, by Adolf Brodsky), where it elicited from the formidable and influential Eduard Hanslick the memorable phrase "stinks in the ear."

It is no wonder, then, that the creative energy of the morbidly sensitive Tchaikovsky, badgered by the critics, still tormented by the persistent echoes of the Antonina affair, and now fearful that his

struggles with Destiny. And in 1869, Tchaikovsky composed *Fatum,* a symphonic poem on a similar theme, based on Konstantin Batyushkov's verses on the futility of life. In this case, the futility extended to the music; on the advice of Mily Balakirev (who included an exhortation to go back and take another look at the Liszt work), Tchaikovsky destroyed the score. (It has been reconstructed and recorded, and isn't all *that* bad.)

He may have destroyed *Fatum,* but the struggle with Fate went on.

The exhortation that comes at the start and end of the *Fourth Symphony,* and the theme that begins the *Fifth* and then intrudes upon all four movements, were all identified by Tchaikovsky as the stern vigil that Fate maintains over us all. Is the triumphant ending of the *Fifth,* with the Fate theme in grand and glorious symphonic array, the victory of Fate over mankind or vice versa? We may never know.

secret lifestyle had become common knowledge, went into a distinct slump. Antonina's demands dogged his waking hours until 1881, when he was finally able to put through a divorce upon his delighted discovery that she had mothered an illegitimate child. He spent as much time away from Moscow as he could, preferring the rural solitude of one of the von Meck estates that had been made available to him, or of his sister's home at Kamenka in the Ukraine. In October 1878, he resigned his post at the Conservatory.

He continued to work, but the compositions of these relatively unproductive "trough" years, roughly 1878-85, seldom recaptured the freshness and daring of the *Fourth Symphony, Romeo and Juliet*, or even the *Piano Concerto* (slowly making its way among Europe's virtuosos),

Eduard Hanslick: Formidable critic best known for his articulate attacks on Wagner.

and lacked as well the sense of personal involvement that makes much of *Eugene Onegin* so heartrending. Occasionally a new score recaptured the depth of feeling of those earlier works: the elegiac *Piano Trio* of 1882, a memorial to Nikolay Rubinstein; and the long and elaborate *Manfred* Symphony of 1885, where the trials and heartaches of Byron's hero resounded in their emotional fullness, almost as a stand-in for Tchaikovsky himself. The *Trio* (written for Nadezhda von Meck's resident chamber ensemble, which at the time included the 20-year-old

Claude Debussy as pianist) seemed to speak with Tchaikovsky's own voice: his genuine grief at the passing of his long-time patron and well-meaning adversary, and a series of charming reminiscences of events in Nikolay's own life.

Late in 1878, Tchaikovsky began an extensive sojourn in the West. In Florence in December, he began an opera on Joan of Arc, which took its title but not much else from Friedrich Schiller's *The Maid of Orleans* and with his own rather contrived libretto that included a love scene between Joan and a Burgundian knight named Lionel. The opera,

Leopold Auer: The great violin virtuoso, teacher (later) of Heifetz, rejected the Tchaikovsky Concerto as unmusical.

first staged in St. Petersburg in 1881, was not well received; only a single aria, Joan's farewell to her beloved forests as she sets out to save her country, maintains the work's popularity today. The *Capriccio Italien*, a delightful pastiche of Italian melodies both authentic and invented, was a more substantial product of the Italy visit, although Tchaikovsky himself had no great affection for the work.

Truth be told, he didn't care much for most of his music during those years, despite its occasional popular acclaim. The *Solemn Overture 1812*, composed for the 1880 Moscow Exhibition, earned a huge ovation (as it does today) but didn't please him at all; a *Piano Sonata* and the *Second Piano Concerto* won only tepid acceptance.

Tchaikovsky as Critic

What is Beethoven—whom it is usual to praise unconditionally and to worship as a god—to me? I bow before the greatness of some of his works, but I do not love Beethoven ...He has made me tremble, but rather from something like fear. I love the middle period...but I fundamentally detest the last, especially the last quartets. Here there are glimmers, nothing more. The rest is chaos, over which, surrounded by an impenetrable fog, hovers the spirit of this musical Jehovah.

> —Diary, 1886

Just as the Abbé Bernini has flooded Rome with his statues, in which he strives to imitate the style of Michelangelo without possessing his genius, so Beethoven's musical style has been copied again and again. Is not Brahms in reality a caricature of Beethoven? Is not this pretension to profundity and power detestable?

> —Letter to Grand Duke Constantin, 1888

The conglomeration of the most complex and refined harmonies, the colorlessness of everything sung on-stage, the endlessly long dialogues...all this is exhausting to the nerves in the extreme. And so this is what Wagner's reform seeks to achieve! Before, music sought to delight people; now they are tormented and exhausted.

> —Letter to Modest from Bayreuth, 1876

I have never been so bored as with Tristan und Isolde.

> —Letter to Nadezhda von Meck, 1882

I would go mad if it weren't for music. It alone clarifies, reconciles and consoles. It is a faithful friend, protector and comforter, and for its sake alone life in this world is worth living. Who knows, perhaps in heaven there will be no music. So let us live on the earth while we still have life!

> —Letter to Nadezhda von Meck, 1881

In September 1882, he completed work on another opera, *Mazeppa,* based on Pushkin's poem *Poltava,* which received concurrent premieres in Moscow and St. Petersburg in February 1884, but no great praise. Nonetheless, the recently crowned Tsar Aleksandr III, a fervent admirer of Tchaikovsky's music, awarded him the Order of St. Vladimir, an honor tantamount to knighthood.

Only one work from this period satisfied the composer's own artistic conscience. He had often voiced his adoration of Mozart's music and, indeed, of the rococo elegance of the earliest works of the Salzburg genius. His 1877 *Variations on a Rococo Theme* for cello and small orchestra embodied this admiration. So now, three years later, did the *Serenade for String Orchestra,* inhabiting a sound world very much akin to an eighteenth-century divertimento—but with a thoroughly nineteenth-century waltz that became its most popular movement. Even Anton Rubinstein, back at the St. Petersburg Conservatory, found it in his heart this once to admire a work of Tchaikovsky's unreservedly.

The tsar's recognition, and the eventual fading from memory of some of the recent traumas, seemed to restore Tchaikovsky's strength. Since 1878, he had wandered somewhat aimlessly, both geographically and musically: in and out of Western Europe, in and out of various hospitable country estates, in and out of musical styles serious and trivial. *Eugene Onegin* was steadily growing in popularity and esteem; he was elected head of the Moscow branch of the

Russian Musical Society; his relationship with his former mentor (and sometime nemesis) Mily Balakirev, which had languished for several years, had been moved to a front burner once again at Balakirev's own request. In February 1885, Tchaikovsky settled down outside Moscow in the village of Maidanovo near Klin. He remained in that region for the rest of his life.

As he had with *Romeo and Juliet*, Balakirev urged Tchaikovsky to consider a musical setting of Byron's *Manfred*, further suggesting that a look at Hector Berlioz' narrative techniques in his *Fantastic* Symphony and *Harold in Italy* might offer some possible models. Balakirev had not lost his persuasive powers; the long, brilliantly orchestrated symphony-in-all-but-name he inspired from his former protégé does, indeed, evoke the fantastic coloristic, story-telling powers of the individualistic French genius, along with a return of the emotional strengths found in the best works of Tchaikovsky himself.

He was not yet out of the woods, however. Late in 1885, comfortable in his Maidanovo lodgings, he worked steadily on a new opera that was also preordained to failure. *The Sorceress* told of the love of a mature widow for a young prince; she is then accused of sorcery, with melodramatic consequences. Despite obvious parallels to his own personal problems, the characters seemed not to have interested Tchaikovsky very much, or elicited music of much distinction. He conducted the first four performances at St. Petersburg in November 1887; the public and critical verdict was almost unanimously negative. One journalist wrote in the *Petersburgskii Listok* of Tchaikovsky's "inability to convey in music the dramatic situation." And the belligerent César Cui, probably mindful of Tchaikovsky's many attacks against the Five, loosed his venom-tipped pen to note that "[Tchaikovsky's] music has little passion, force or energy, and it was easy to guess that the dramatic scenes in his new opera would not be satisfactory..." Tchaikovsky's skin was not yet toughened against such slings and arrows; he took the work's failure very badly. "On no other opera," he wrote to Nadezhda von Meck, "have I ever labored so or exerted such effort, and at the same time never before have I been the object of such persecution on the part of the press."

Before this fiasco Tchaikovsky interrupted his work for a month's sojourn at Tbilisi, in the province of Georgia. There he was feted by local musicians, and got to introduce, at long last, the final revision of *Romeo and Juliet* which he had completed in 1880, six years before. Now, with *The Sorceress* behind him, he set out on his first foreign tour as a conductor. In

Tchaikovsky's garden: The house at Klin was a blessed refuge. Tchaikovsky's brother Modest took it over after Pyotr's death, and fashioned it into a museum.

Germany he made the acquaintance of Brahms and Grieg, and also had a brief but pleasant reunion with Désirée Artôt. Despite his previously published dislike for Brahms' *First Symphony,* the meeting between the two men was cordial, with Brahms—himself a fair match for Tchaikovsky in the shyness department—successfully breaking down his colleague's reserve.

Tchaikovsky returned in April 1888, and moved into a larger house close by his former residence. And although he claimed to take greater pleasure in his garden than his writing table, he started work on a *Fifth Symphony.*

CHAPTER 6

The Bitter End

NIKOLAY KONDRYATIN HAD BEEN one of Tchaikovsky's closest friends since their school days in St. Petersburg; the two had kept their ties strong even amid the whirling circles of Moscow's homosexual life. Afflicted for years with the consequences of badly treated syphilis—the cure, involving high doses of mercury, was frequently more deadly than the disease—Kondryatin went to Aachen in the summer of 1887 to take the therapeutic waters there. It was apparently to no avail. Tchaikovsky himself was at the spa at Borzhom in the Caucasus when a telegram arrived from Aachen, begging him to come to Kondryatin's side. Tchaikovsky spent more than a month watching his friend die, torn between his longtime love and disgust at the spectacle of the tormented, wasted body. "Painful, terrible hours!" he wrote to Modest. "Never will I forget all that I have suffered here!"

Sketching the *Fifth Symphony* in Tiblis in April 1888, Tchaikovsky was still haunted by his experience at Kondryatin's deathbed eight months before. His earliest notebook sketches outline a program: "Introduction: complete submission before fate...before the inscrutable predestination of Providence. Allegro: murmur of doubt, complaints, reproaches...No, no hope!" These entries suggest a soul in deep crisis.

He began actual work on the symphony in May. He thought constantly of Kondryatin. Walking in the park at Maidanovo, he found everything "melancholy and sad; nowhere else have I experienced so vividly the grief of Kondryatin's departure..." Work on the symphony went slowly, interrupted by bouts of illness either real or psychosomatic—and also by random forays to Moscow or St. Petersburg to sample the nightlife along the cities' riverbanks and to fall in love perhaps two or three times a night. Despite all this, the work was essentially complete by mid-August, and Tchaikovsky had already launched a new project, a *Hamlet* overture that would serve as a companion to *Romeo and Juliet* and *The Tempest*.

The new symphony was mildly received at first; the acid pen of César Cui described it as a triumph of "sound over music." Tchaikovsky's own conducting of the work was probably at fault; as he gained command of its convoluted ways on the podium, public recognition of the *Fifth Symphony* seemed to grow accordingly. Even Johannes Brahms, who had attended a dress rehearsal in Hamburg,

Tchaikovsky in Hamburg, 1888, at the first performance there of the Fifth Symphony.

approved of most of the work; only the finale seemed to him inferior.

Back home in December after a time in St. Petersburg and Prague—where he presented both the new symphony and the *Second Piano Concerto* (with the pianist Vasily Sapelnikov, whose 1920s recording of the *First Concerto,* miraculously, still circulates)— Tchaikovsky immediately began work on a new ballet, *The Sleeping Beauty,* for the great choreographer Marius Petipa and his troupe at St. Petersburg's Maryinsky Theater. The scenario called for magical effects, and Tchaikovsky fulfilled them with magic of his own; *The Sleeping Beauty* is generally rated the finest of his three major ballet scores. The ballet had its premiere in January 1890; Tchaikovsky left directly for Florence, where the Italian sun warmed his spirit. There he labored primarily on a new opera, based on Aleksandr Pushkin's gripping short story with supernatural overtones, *Pikovaya dama* (*The Queen of Spades*). It was commissioned by the tenor Nikolay Figner and his wife, Medea. The story so engrossed Tchaikovsky that he had the work fully sketched in about six weeks. A string sextet called *Souvenir de Florence* also dates from the Florence sojourn, as robust and extroverted as *The Queen of Spades* was gloom-filled and mysterious.

Tchaikovsky was now well-off. The citation from Aleksandr III carried with it a yearly stipend of 3,000 rubles; a nice complement to the 6,000 from Nadezhda von Meck and his fair income from royalties and conducting engagements. Nevertheless, a note from von Meck in October 1890, disturbed him greatly. Her finances were in disarray, she claimed (although this was later found to be false), and she had to discontinue Tchaikovsky's subsidy. Tchaikovsky did not need the money; what saddened him was that von Meck seemed anxious to break off their relationship completely. Tchaikovsky's letters to her now went unanswered. The realization that their fourteen years of correspondence, into which both had poured page after page of intense self-confession—the composer also contributing the wisdom of an outspoken participant in their country's cultural life—might have been for her only a pleasant diversion, left him once again crushed and embittered.

There was, at least, one more great passion to raise his spirits: Vladimir Lvovich Davïdov, known as Bob, the one son of his sister Aleksandra who aroused Tchaikovsky's love both as uncle and admirer. As early as 1884, at the age of thirteen, Bob's charms had found their mark, and his uncle's gushing reports to the ever-understanding Modest constitute virtually a play-by-play account of their growing closeness. "Bobik plays a large role in my life here," he confided. "Formerly he only allowed himself to be adored, while now he seems to have begun to value my adoration. And I do adore him, the longer the more powerfully..."

The adoration ripened into abiding friendship; Bob was to serve as good right hand, confidante, traveling companion, and, doubtless, lover for the rest of his uncle's life; he was awarded a fair portion of Tchaikovsky's estate in his will. He was the dedicatee of the composer's last work, the *Pathétique* Symphony. He did not, however, fulfill Tchaikovsky's high hopes for his artistic success, and in 1906, at the age of 34, he died from a self-inflicted bullet wound.

In March 1891, Tchaikovsky embarked on his first and only American conquest—he had been invited to conduct his music during the ceremonies inaugurating New York's new music hall, built from the benefice of the steel magnate Andrew Carnegie and later to bear his name. Tchaikovsky left Europe in a state of despair; his beloved sister Aleksandra had recently died. New York terrified him, despite the kindness and respect extended to him by Americans. If his diary entries are to be believed, every day of his two weeks in New York was punctuated by frequent spells of weeping. "American manners are very attractive to me," he wrote, "but I enjoy this like a person at a table set with marvels of gastronomy, devoid of appetite. Only the prospect of returning to Russia can awaken an appetite within me." He admired the skyscrapers; visited Niagara Falls and Washington, D.C.; conducted parts of four concerts in New York and two in Philadelphia and Baltimore; and returned to Russia (via Hamburg) as fast as he could. His four appearances in New York had earned him $2500, considered a handsome sum at the time.

Tchaikovsky's last years were marked by increasing world acclaim and increasing inner anguish. A commission from St.

Tchaikovsky in New York

From *The Life and Letters of Tchaikovsky* by Modest Tchaikovsky:

Day 1, April 27, 1891, Letter to Modest. "The nearer we came to New York, the greater grew my fear and homesickness...I was met by four very amiable gentlemen and a lady, who took me straight to the Hotel Normandie. After [they] had gone I began to walk up and down my rooms and shed many tears...I went for a stroll down Broadway. An extraordinary street! Houses of one and two stories alternate with some nine-storied buildings. Most original. I was struck with the number of nigger faces I saw..."

Day 4, April 30, Letter to Bob Davïdov. "New York, American customs, American hospitality—everything is to my taste. If only I were younger I should very much enjoy my visit to this interesting and youthful country. But now I just tolerate everything as a slight punishment mitigated by many pleasant things. I am convinced that I am ten times more famous in America than in Europe."

Diary. "...The houses down town are simply colossal. I do not understand how anyone can live on the thirteenth floor."

Petersburg resulted in two works designed to constitute a longish double bill, but now consigned to separate lives. One part was *Iolanta* (*Iolanthe*, but unrelated to the Gilbert and Sullivan operetta), a fairy-tale opera set in Provence telling of a blind girl whose sight is restored through love; charming and ingratiating, if a rather simple work to follow *The Queen of Spades*. The other part was to score a ballet created by Petipa out of the E.T.A. Hoffmann story of a toy nutcracker

Day 9, May 5 (inaugural of the new Music Hall), diary. "The appearance of the hall in the evening, lit up and crowded with people, was very fine and effective. The ceremony began with a speech. After this the National Anthem [actually, the hymn "Old Hundredth"] was sung. Then a clergyman made a long and wearisome speech...The Leonore Symphony [Overture No. 3] was beautifully rendered. Interval. I appeared, and was greeted with loud applause. The March ["Marche solennelle," which Tchaikovsky conducted at the inaugural concert] went splendidly. Great success."

Day 12, May 8, diary. "Visitors without end, among others two Russian ladies... This was the first time I had had the pleasure of speaking to a Russian lady; consequently, I made a fool of myself. Suddenly tears came into my eyes, my voice broke and I could not suppress my sobs. I fled into the next room..."

Niagara Falls, Day 16, May 12, diary. " I will not try to describe the beauty of the Falls; it is hard to find words for such things."

Day 24, the final day, May 20. "At eight o'clock I was taken to the Composers' Club. In the middle of the evening I received an address; I answered shortly, in French. One lady threw an exquisite bouquet of roses straight in my face..."

and his battles with the forces of the Mouse King. This, too, elicited light-weight music; Tchaikovsky himself thought the ballet far below *Swan Lake* or *The Sleeping Beauty*. Yet *The Nutcracker* has amassed a performance history surely greater than any other

Tchaikovsky's drawing room: The spacious main room at the composer's house in Klin.

dance creation, and the suite fashioned by Tchaikovsky in 1892 remains his most frequently played music.

He continued his travels, including conducting engagements in Warsaw and Paris during 1892 and a visit to England to pick up an honorary doctorate at Cambridge University. Late in 1892, he nearly completed a new symphony in the key of E flat, but grew dissatisfied with the music and converted the first movement into the one-movement *Piano Concerto No. 3*, a failure.

Returning from one of his journeys, he hit upon an idea for another large-scale score, a "Programme Symphony" as he called it. Sometime in 1892, he scribbled some notes: "First movement, all impulsive passion, confidence, thirst for activity. Second movement, love; third, disappointments; fourth ends dying away..." By August 1893, the work was completed, dedicated to Bob Davïdov; it was first performed in St. Petersburg on 28 October. The day after the premiere, Modest suggested the title *Pathétique*.

The symphony was Tchaikovsky's last work, and by some distance his most pessimistic. The first movement, enormous in its breadth of emotion, climbs out of an almost inaudible dark cloud of tone to reach the passionate outburst of its second theme—which later joined the company of bankable Tchaikovsky tunes on Tin Pan Alley under the title "The Story of a Starry Night." The second movement is a kind of waltz, but in the unusual meter of 5/4. (In one of his more egregious howlers, the usually infallible Eduard Hanslick protested that the movement "could without the least inconvenience be arranged in 6/8"). The third movement, the place of the scherzo, is taken up in a thunderous, sardonic, and brilliantly-scored march, which invariably draws applause before the finale breaks the mood with its deep outlay of despair, climaxing with a single stroke on the gong that seems like a faint light flashing from another planet.

Nine days after the work's premiere, on 6 November 1893, Tchaikovsky died, in his 54th year. A veritable basketful of stories have been advanced to account for his demise. Russia was in the grip of a cholera epidemic; did Tchaikovsky bring on his death by purposely drinking a glass of unboiled water? Did he thus flaunt health measures to show his defiance of death? Was it an act of suicide—or foolishness? Was it, as one highly elaborate story has it, the result of his swallowing arsenic on the order of a high Russian official with whose nephew Tchaikovsky had dallied? All stories, and none, are entirely plausible or implausible. The fact of Tchaikovsky's death is spelled out most clearly in the final minutes of the "Pathétique" Symphony. Anything else is extraneous matter.

By the time of his death, Tchaikovsky was an exponent of a musical outlook already old-fashioned and going out of style—at least in the view of progressive circles in the West and even in the United States. By 1893 Gustav Mahler had composed five of his ten symphonies; Claude Debussy was revising his *Prelude to the*

One Man's Poison

The shadowy world of gossip, innuendo, and blackmail in which Tchaikovsky spent most of his life did not end with his death. Almost immediately rumors began to circulate—he had killed himself out of depression over the poor reception of the *Pathétique* Symphony (which did no harm to the growing fame of the work), or in answer to an ultimatum from Aleksandr III, concerned that rumors of Tchaikovsky's various dalliances involved members of his court. In November 1980, an émigrée musicologist, Alexandra

Orlova, published her new "findings" in a New York Russian-language paper: Tchaikovsky had been called to trial by a panel of his former schoolmates at the School of Jurisprudence who were fearful that his proclivities might sully the school, and was handed a dose of arsenic with orders to take it. This account made it into the Tchaikovsky entries of at least two reputable references: the *Encyclopedia Britannica* and the *New Grove Dictionary*.

Every known and official detail of Tchaikovsky's death contradicts her story. If the panel was really dedicated to saving the reputation

Afternoon of a Faun after its first performance the year before; Charles Ives had driven his Yale professors up the wall with his variations on "America" that went through several keys; Scott Joplin had gone north from Sedalia, Missouri to the Columbian Exposition in Chicago, where an older composer had taught him how to write things down.

Yet Tchaikovsky's music persisted, and at least one more generation of Russian composers would keep alive the practice of amalgamating the formal outlines of the traditional symphony with the

of the school by killing off its homosexual alumni, at least half of its graduates would have committed suicide by 1893. The symptoms of cholera that ravaged Tchaikovsky's body differed from the effect of arsenic or any other poison. The timing of their appearance and recurrence also contradicts another fanciful story: that Tchaikovsky defied the health rules of the cholera epidemic by drinking a glass of unboiled water at a dinner party he attended the night before his collapse (if he did imbibe, his distress would not have occured so soon). It has been confirmed that Tchaikovsky's doctors delayed their treatment unnecessarily through a breakdown in communications, but this may have been the composer's fault. Hot baths, commonly employed to relieve the symptoms of cholera, had been used by his mother just before she died of the disease, and his letters underscore his morbid dread of the treatment.

Tchaikovsky died at a time of greater fame and acclaim than he had ever enjoyed, happy in the love of his nephew Bob Davïdov, and with his worktable filled with new projects. Bringing about his own death was not one of them.

lushness of Slavic melodies—a generation that included Sergey Rachmaninoff, Aleksandr Glazunov, and Vasily Kallinikov in Russia, and sent its messages abroad to an eager nationalist in the nearby Finnish territory, Jean Sibelius.

Russian music was greatly assisted in its global conquest by the scores of native virtuosos who found audiences swooning at their feet in Rio de Janeiro, San Francisco, Boston, and every European music center. Rachmaninoff himself toured the world; so did violinists Mischa Elman and Jascha Heifetz, and the spellbinding basso Fyodor Chaliapin. By the 1920s, the sensational Serge Koussevitzky—whose publishing house in Paris had made scores and parts of Russian music, both conservative and wild, accessible worldwide—had come to America to conduct the Boston Symphony Orchestra.

The music of Tchaikovsky's contemporaries also survived—the ardent, nationalistic musical panoramas by the members of the Five, avowed opponents in theory of Tchaikovsky's "Germanic" influences, but admiring colleagues once his fame had outstripped theirs. Their great, sloppy, innovative operas drawn from Russian history—Mussorgsky's *Boris Godunov* and Borodin's *Prince Igor*

Modest Mussorgsky: This famous portrait comes from Mussorgsky's last years; it seems to reflect the madness of Boris Godunov, from Mussorgsky's most famous opera.

Stravinsky on Tchaikovsky

"Tchaikovsky possessed the power of *melody,* center of gravity in every symphony, opera or ballet composed by him. It is absolutely indifferent to me that the quality of his melody was sometimes unequal. The fact is that he was a creator of melody, which is a rare and precious gift...something that is not German."

> —*Igor Stravinsky's open letter to Sergey Diaghilev, published in the London* Times, *18 October 1921*

No later countryman more honored Tchaikovsky's music than Igor Stravinsky. Even though he lived most of his life as an expatriate, his boyhood adoration of the older composer—he was eleven at the time of Tchaikovsky's death—never left him. In his early years as a conductor, Stravinsky led performances worldwide of Tchaikovsky's *Second, Third,* and *Pathétique* symphonies; later on, when his programs were mostly devoted to his own music, the Tchaikovsky *Second* was still frequently on the bill.

Stravinsky composed his ballet *The Fairy's Kiss* in 1928; it was first performed by the Ballets Ida Rubinstein at the Paris Opéra that November. The music was drawn from the works of its dedicatee, Tchaikovsky: piano pieces and songs, all transmogrified by Stravinsky's own sense of rhythm and harmony. Tchaikovsky's hand is everywhere apparent, but Stravinsky's assimilation of the Tchaikovskian melos is complete. "Instead of being Tchaikovsky's inevitable squares," wrote Stravinsky biographer Lawrence Morton, referring to the sharp shifts and edges in Stravinsky's music, "they are Stravinsky's rhomboids, scalenes, trapeziums or trapezoids... Tchaikovsky's faults are composed *out* of the music, and Stravinsky's virtues are composed *into* it."

Aleksandr Borodin (1833-1887): A chemist and self-taught composer, Borodin was another member of the Five, best known for his opera Prince Igor.

most notably—took their place in the international repertory, with a little help from Rimsky-Korsakov's editing. (Rimsky's operas themselves seem to be coming into their own now, a century after their composition—a wildly colorful collection of fairy-tale pieces they are, too.)

The heart-on-sleeve style of the great Tchaikovsky melodies secure his reputation, even when the glue turns sticky: the love theme from *Romeo and Juliet*, the horn solo in the *Fifth Symphony*, the big tune in the first movement of the *Pathétique*, the "Tonight We Love" theme that starts the *Piano Concerto* (and never returns), Tatyana's outpourings in the Letter Scene from *Eugene Onegin*—the list goes on and on. But this does not convey the full panoply of his singular genius. The first movements of the *Fifth* and *Sixth* symphonies display a remarkable insight into the way the outlines of the classical **sonata form**—the same outlines that had served Mozart and Beethoven so well—could be turned into a powerful nonverbal drama. Just the sounds of Tchaikovsky—the prismatic glints in the *Nutcracker* music or the scherzo for pizzicato strings in the *Fourth Symphony*, the black-on-black colorations at the start and end of the *Pathétique*—are effects no other composer provides.

His music outlived the vagaries of Russian and Soviet political proscriptions, as readily as it outlives its treatment by the dance bands, its being danced to by goldfish and mushrooms courtesy of the Disney Studios, or when a symphony gets to be sung as a fake opera by Nelson and Jeanette. Just that lasting power is enough to secure Tchaikovsky a place among the immortals.

CHAPTER 7

Tchaikovsky: Play by Play

IT WAS LUDWIG VAN BEETHOVEN who, in his monumental *Ninth Symphony,* clearly implied that the orchestral symphony as an abstract concept had gone about as far as it could go—that music's path extended toward a much closer involvement with human joys, sorrows, and outcries, rather than the pure designs that Mozart and Haydn had carried to a plane of eloquence—and that the symphony of the future had to be *about* something. Six decades after Beethoven's prime, Pyotr Ilich Tchaikovsky tended to talk or write about his symphonies not so much in terms of classical structure, but as reflections of the role fate played in the affairs of humans, the shadow cast over our earthly lives by destiny's determining. (Fate and the Slavic sensibility have always formed a seamless union; the force of destiny far outweighs any action by mere mortals. Was it mere coincidence that Giuseppe

Verdi's opera by that name, *La forza del destino*, had been composed for the St. Petersburg Opera and had had its world premiere in that city in 1862?)

Not all symphonies after Beethoven, of course, culminated with singers crying out to reject all that instrumental stuff and sail into a grand choral apotheosis; that happened only sporadically, as with Franz Liszt's *Faust* Symphony, until Gustav Mahler's *Second Symphony* of 1888 opened the floodgates for the anything-goes symphony of late Romanticism. Johannes Brahms kept the spirit of the abstract, classical symphonic forms alive; so, indeed, did Tchaikovsky's one compatriot with symphonic inclinations, the chemist and part-time composer Aleksandr Borodin. But Beethoven's *Ninth Symphony* had spoken its piece, proposing the notion of symphony as narrative; that the four or five movements of an orchestral work need no longer be set apart from one another in the classical pattern of contrasts and balances, but that they could be linked by underlying musical and literary devices in order to carry an action forward toward its resolution.

Hector Berlioz wrote the *Fantastic* Symphony only three years after Beethoven's death. In that work of extraordinary bravery, a theme devised to personify the composer's love-object, hovering continually just out of reach, undergoes musical changes from one movement to another until at the end "she" turns up at a witches' Sabbath. In his *Faust* Symphony, Franz Liszt gave each of his principals—

Faust, Gretchen, and Mephistopheles—a recognizable tune, so that listeners could follow their activities from one moment to the next guided by the changes in their musical themes. And the prototype of this notion of tracing a narrative through the varying physiognomies in the musical depiction of its major characters occurred not in a symphony, but in the huge *Ring of the Nibelungen* by Richard Wagner, where every character and philosophical concept had a calling card or *leitmotiv* capable of infinite coloration.

Tchaikovsky had already demonstrated his mastery of the orchestral narrative in the 1870 *Romeo and Juliet Fantasy-Overture* and the 1880 *Overture 1812*. In both works, the themes assigned to the protagonists—Romeo, Juliet, Friar Laurence, the French and Russian armies—tell their stories vividly by means of musical metamorphosis. In the *Fourth Symphony,* too, there are hints of an overarching "program" that gives the work some kind of narrative shape; the stentorian, summoning theme that begins the work bursts out once more right at the climax of the finale—truly a message of considerable weight, if unspecified import. In 1888, he applied his storytelling powers to a truly narrative symphony. Its opening theme, which Tchaikovsky acknowledged as a "complete submission before Fate—or, what is the same thing, the inscrutable design of Providence" shows up in all four movements, undergoing a change of costume in each. (He took the theme itself from Mikhail Glinka's opera *A Life for the Tsar*, where, in a trio in the first act, it accompanies the words "turn not into sorrow.") The transformation of the Fate theme is hardly subtle, but it makes its dramatic point nonetheless—from its solemn, even somewhat sullen, first appearance in the most funereal depths of the orchestra's wind section (and in the key of woe minor) to the striding E-major apotheosis at the end, with pauses along the way to shake its fist at all young, moonstruck lovers in the slow movement and to mutter a further warning from out of the shadows near the end of the waltz.

Tchaikovsky worked on his *Fifth Symphony* in the summer of 1888 at his new country home at Frolovskoe, not far outside Moscow in a picturesque setting on a wooded hill. Tchaikovsky loved the place; the simple, rolling landscape was dearer to him, he wrote, than all the mountain vistas of Switzerland and Italy. Yet the vista was doomed; within three years after he moved there the surrounding forest had begun to succumb to the real estate developer's ax—the fate memorialized in Chekhov's *The Cherry Orchard.* Tchaikovsky moved on; a month before his death, heading toward Moscow, he looked out at the churchyard of Frolovskoe. "I should like to be buried there," he told his traveling companion.

By that summer he was certain that the mental depression that had slowed his pen in previous years was now conquered. "I shall work my hardest," he wrote to Mme. von Meck on 22 June 1888. "I am exceedingly anxious to prove to myself, as to others, that I am not played out as a composer. Have I told you that I intend to write a symphony? The beginning was difficult, but now inspiration seems to have come. We shall see..." The symphony was completed in August, and Tchaikovsky led performances in St. Petersburg and Prague, well received by audiences but not by critics. "One vainly sought for coherence and homogeneity...the Valse [waltz] was a piece of musical padding, commonplace to a degree," wrote the *Musical Courier*'s European correspondent.

"I have come to the conclusion that [the *Fifth Symphony*] is a failure," Tchaikovsky wrote to Mme. von Meck in December. "There is something repellent, something superfluous, patchy and insincere which the public instinctively recognizes." One fault the composer seems not to have recognized: his own inadequacy as a conductor. Eventually, as the conductor Tchaikovsky acquired greater mastery over the composer Tchaikovsky, the new symphony earned its rightful success; at the Hamburg premiere in early 1889, both musicians and the public demonstrated their enthusiasm. Even the implacable Johannes Brahms, whom Tchaikovsky had first met in a rather stiff encounter in Hamburg a year before and happened to be in the city again, stayed on an extra day expressly to hear the final rehearsals of the *Fifth Symphony*. He expressed a grudging approval of the work, except for its finale. But then, there wasn't much in his contemporaries' music that Brahms *did* admire.

The *Fifth Symphony* bears a dedication to Count Ave-Lallemant, chairman of the Committee of the Hamburg Philharmonic Society, who had befriended Tchaikovsky earlier. "This venerable old man of over eighty paid me great attention," Tchaikovsky noted in his diary. "Herr Lallemant candidly confessed that many of my works that had been performed in Hamburg were not to his taste; he could not endure my noisy orchestration and disliked my use of instruments of percussion. Almost with tears in his eyes he besought me to leave Russia and settle permanently in Germany, where classical conventions and traditions of high culture could not fail to correct my faults, which were easily explainable by the fact of my having been born and educated in a country so unenlightened and so far behind Germany…We parted good friends."

Perhaps this explains why the *Fifth Symphony,* alone among Tchaikovsky's mature orchestral works, contains no "instruments of percussion" aside from the traditional set of kettledrums.

Symphony No. 5 in E minor, Opus 64

Scoring: *pairs of flutes (plus piccolo), oboes, clarinets, bassoons, and trumpets. Four horns, three trombones (plus tuba), and timpani, strings. Dedication: Count Ave-Lallemant. Completed in 1888; first public performance, 17 November 1888, St. Petersburg.*

First Movement: ***Andante,* leading to *allegro con anima***

Introduction: *Andante*

Over a measured, funereal tread in the low strings, the clarinets sound the Fate theme [let's call it "(X)" in its many reappearances and reworkings throughout the movements of the symphony]. The theme breaks down into two parts, and each of these consists of two phrases which are sometimes dealt with as separate entities. (X1) **[T1/i1, 0:00]** is the very spirit of pessimism; (X2) **[T1/i1, 0:16]** perpetuates the blahs with a couple of downward-sliding scales in which the strings form a bleak aura around the clarinets. The answering phrase **[T1/i1, 0:40]** takes the whole sequence further up on the scale, albeit without making matters any more hopeful. This entire woebegone paragraph constitutes the central figure of the drama; we will encounter bits and pieces of it as the symphony moves along, until the entire passage returns in blazing triumph near the end, some fifty minutes from now.

> *This is the time to mention Dr. Sigmund Spaeth, who once hosted a radio program called* The Tune Detective *and also published several books aimed at attracting young people to classical music. In a book entitled* Great Symphonies and How to Recognize Them *(long out of print) he dreamed up the idea of writing "lyrics" to the most popular themes. The lyrics don't necessarily relate to the mood of the music itself, but even so, they can be helpful memory devices. Theme X: "Glory to God in the highest, glory to God in his Heaven, and peace on Earth to men." Theme A: "Then rally around in the cause of mankind; we'll start today the way to find." Theme C: "Onward, onward, onward, onward!" Get the idea?*

(X1) sounds again **[T1/i1, 1:22]** and again **[T1/i1, 1:34]**, supported by the bassoons in their most mournful register, landing with each repetition on a new and more disturbing **harmony**. (X2) prolongs the sense of expectation **[T1/i1, 2:15]**. The music hangs suspended; it has not been a happy time so far.

Exposition: *Allegro con anima*

The pace has quickened, but the sense of foreboding lingers. The clarinets remain out front, and the strings continue their measured tread. Theme (A) **[T1/i2, 2:36]** is hardly more jolly than the Fate motive—until the flutes take it up **[T1/i2, 2:55]**; then there is a noticeable lightening of the cloud cover. At many points in this movement (A) recurs, not in the melodic shape of this first appearance but merely in its distinctive rhythmic outline: "ta TUM-ta-ta TUM-ta-ta tum tum ta tum" (or, as Dr. Spaeth put it: "Then RAL-ly around in the CAUSE of mankind.") Keep it in mind.

> *Tchaikovsky adored the music of Mozart; his frequent diary entries and letters attest to this. And while there is an undeniable gap between the sound of Mozart's orchestra and Tchaikovsky's, there are moments in the Russian composer's work that clearly point to his admiration for the sound spectrum of the Salzburg genius. This brief episode is one, the few seconds of interplay between flutes and clarinets, standing out in clear contrast to the mournful sounds up to now. It stretches no point to suggest that Tchaikovsky's skill at wind scoring rivals Mozart's. Proof? The trio of the scherzo in the* Fourth Symphony, *anywhere you look in the* Nutcracker *music, and, on a more somber*

note, the chamber-music-like interplay between strings and winds at the start of Romeo and Juliet.

Strings take up (A) **[T1/i2, 3:07]** in the principal key of E minor, with the first violins out front for the first time in the work, with clarinets and bassoons slithering deliciously in the background and small points of light from flutes and oboes and an attempt at derailment via a rude three-note figure (TUM-ta-tum) from the horns **[T1/i2, 3:19]**. (A) makes a series of efforts to be heard, louder and louder with a great deal of activity in the winds **[T1/i2, 3:23]**, but that "derailing" figure keeps interrupting. A gruff expostulation from the full orchestra **[T1/i2, 3:46]** leads to an extended battle, with bits and pieces of (A) passing through the orchestra and a buildup of tension toward a major stopping point **[T1/i3, 4:06]**.

A new theme, (B), in the related key of B minor contrasting in its smoother, more lyrical flow, with a poignant, pure-Tchaikovskian sigh at the cadence, is stated by the strings **[T1/i3, 4:27]** with glistening answers from the winds. The winds take up (B) **[T1/i3, 4:55]** over an accompanying figure of descending scale passages (a familiar Tchaikovskian gambit); it fades away to near-silence **[T1/i3, 5:06]**.

A pizzicato "ping" brings on yet another theme, (C), ("Onward, onward...") **[T1/i4, 5:23]** in the key of D major (the relative major of the preceding B minor, but quite distant from the principal key of E minor)—more tranquil than anything we have yet encountered, set as a dialogue between winds and horns (another Mozartian moment) and strings. But there's more to the new theme than just that bouncy, "onward, onward" opening phrase; a consequent answering **melody [T1/i5, 5:47]**, rises heavenward: winds and strings in densely-textured conversation, in a lavish outpouring, becoming increasingly urgent **[T1/i5, 6:24]**. The orchestral brass bring on reminiscences of (A) **[T1/i5, 6:35]**, which plays off in **counterpoint** against (C) and works up a fearsome climax.

> *The musical form known as the "symphony" had already been in existence for 150 years when Tchaikovsky was in his prime. In its classical shape it consisted of three or four movements contrasting in mood, key, pace, and, of course, in content. The classical ideal suggested an exquisite balance between structural unity and the need for contrast; its trail through the eighteenth and early nineteenth centuries is dotted with the masterpieces of Haydn, Mozart, Beethoven, and Schubert. The romantic ideal embodied different attitudes. The neat divisions of the classical symphony—fast movement, slow movement, minuet, finale, exposition, development, recapitulation—gave way to a more continuous musical flow, a striving for oneness. Robert Schumann fashioned his symphonies so that one movement flowed into the next without pause. (Actually, Beethoven had already tried this in his* Fifth *and* Sixth *symphonies.) Franz Liszt's "symphonic poems" bore traces of the old divisions, but were musically continuous.*

> *Within the individual parts of the symphony, a similar continuity seemed to represent important new goals. In a Mozart movement in sonata-form, there was contrast between relatively stable sections (exposition, recapitulation) in which the tonality remained constant*

and the development, which usually employed frequent key change. But as composers late in the nineteenth century explored richer harmonies and more startling dissonances, contrasts between stable and unstable tonalities became less clearly defined, and so did the divisions within a movement. It's easy to discern the sections in Tchaikovsky's Fifth Symphony, *but less easy to relate them to the outlines of a classical pattern. Other considerations—the sense of dramatic narrative, or the irregular unfolding of a melodic pattern—became more important. Some composers after Tchaikovsky—Anton Bruckner, for example—continued to honor the traditional outlines; others—Gustav Mahler, among others—did not.*

Development

The fury dies down, leaving only echoes in the winds and brass of the "onward, onward" phrase from (C) **[T1/i6, 7:01]**. Against this the strings ramble on with a flowing, quiet variant of the rhythmic outline ("Then rally around in the cause of mankind," quoth Dr. Spaeth) of (A) **[T1/i7, 7:16]**. The entire development section—quite short, at two-and-a-half minutes out of the total of sixteen for the entire movement—becomes a ramble, mostly quiet, through the themes of the exposition. (Compare this with a typical Beethoven or Brahms development, where the material of the movement often reaches a tense, sometimes chaotic climax in the development.)

The combination of (A) and (C) works itself up to something of a froth **[T1/i7, 7:53]**. The rhythm of (A) throbs obsessively, and continues as (B) sneaks in under it [T1/i8, 8:09], but only briefly. The rhythm of (A) continues; listen to the way Tchaikovsky spreads it out through the winds [T1/i9, 8:23]; combined once again with the "onward, onward" of (C) [T1/i9, 8:32] it musters a powerful head of steam, with the rhythmic figures echoed back and forth among the orchestral sections and finally subsiding almost to silence.

Recapitulation

Theme (A) is restated as it was at the start of the exposition [T1/i10, 9:21=2:36], but with changes in the orchestration; it comes in first as a bassoon solo, and the answer from the flutes [T1/i10, 9:40] is now an octave higher than before. For most of its duration, the recapitulation does indeed "recapitulate" the order of events from the exposition, but with the key-relations altered so as to bring us back to E minor at the end. (B) returns, this time in C-sharp minor [T1/i11, 10:36=4:27]. A new sequence of key changes leads eventually to a return of (C) [T1/i12, 11:33=5:23] in its Mozartian dialogue between winds and strings—and of its soulful second strain [T1/i12, 11:56=5:47]. As before, this builds up to some powerful orchestral rhetoric, including the dramatic counterpoint of (A) and (C) played off against one another [T1/i13, 12:24=6:24], subsiding as the horns engage in a reminiscence of (C), as they had done at the end of the exposition [T1/i14, 13:10=7:01].

Coda

As if in an inexorable, menacing procession, an urgent variant of (A) strides through the orchestra **[T1/i15, 13:30]**, euphoric for the moment but not for long, as it reaches a new defiant outbreak **[T1/i15, 13:48]**. The throbbing rhythm of (A) persists as the procession seems to vanish toward the horizon until it becomes enveloped in dark shadows. At that point **[T1/i15, 14:12]** nothing remains but the sustained tone of the bassoons in their lowest register, a faint roar on the timpani, and the cellos and basses redefine the glum mood in which the movement began fifteen minutes ago.

Second movement: ***Andante cantabile, con alcuna licenza***
                  (Medium-slow and song-like, with some freedom)

A familiar Tchaikovsky gambit opens this much-loved movement: a slow-moving, chorale-like chord progression through lush, attention-grabbing harmonic twists and turns (compare it to the opening of the *Romeo and Juliet* overture). In this case, the progression seems to tie together the first and second movements of the symphony. The first chord, in B-minor **[T2/i1, 0:00]**, could easily be the consequence of the dark closing of the preceding movement. This time, however, the progression eventually swings around to D major, where it serves as background for (A), the famous horn solo.

Tchaikovsky takes very much to heart the "with some freedom" tempo indication at the start of the movement. The horn solo **[T2/i1, 0:56]** is further marked *dolce con molto espressione* ("sweet, with much expression") and is peppered with dynamic indications and exhortations to speed up and slacken the pace—all within the space of eight bars. (Dr. Spaeth finds patriotism, not "moon love" in the theme: "tell ev'ry nation, all of creation...") A solo clarinet joins the horn for the second strain of the melody [T2/i1, 1:47]. The clarinet is replaced by a solo oboe, as a new (B) ("hope springs anew, dreams will come true" in Dr. Spaeth's rendition) ensues without a break [T2/i2, 2:32] over throbbing triplets in the strings. Horn, oboe, and clarinet fade away [T2/i2, 2:47], and the low strings echo the final phrases of the new melody.

Led by the violas, the music returns to (A) in an elegant, transparent new orchestration [T2/i3, 3:15]; winds and strings weave a garland of melodic lines around the principal theme, and the score once again is punctuated with directions to speed up, slow down, and vary the dynamics. The music turns more urgent [T2/i3, 3:48] and pushes forward with considerably greater force than before. (B) bursts forth in the full orchestra [T2/i4, 4:13] and grows toward a mighty climax [T2/i4, 4:57], a fortississimo (*fff*) declaration of the theme. This quickly subsides, however, and the mood becomes mysterious [T2/i5, 5:14] as the winds—solo clarinet, two bassoons, then flutes and oboes—sing a spacious, haunting new theme (C) (no word from Dr. Spaeth), answered with poignant passion by the strings. The theme repeats [T2/i5, 6:44] with a sense of greater restlessness, an urgency to move ahead. The strings build up the forward energy

[T2/i5, 6:57] toward something that promises to be cataclysmic.

And so it is, a mighty explosion in the brass as the Fate melody (X1 and X2) shatters the atmosphere **[T2/i6, 7:22]** and just as suddenly vanishes, leaving the strings to regain their composure as best they can **[T2/i7, 8:01]**. (A) flows forth once again, in a beautifully scored dialogue between the violins and a solo oboe **[T2/i7, 8:12]**. The clarinets add further embroidery around the theme **[T2/i7, 8:26]**: what marvelous, flowing, flickering orchestration! The pace quickens, and so does the orchestral activity **[T2/i7, 8:46]**. Another huge buildup materializes, as the orchestra leaves no stone unturned in its zeal to underline the passion of this theme **[T2/i7, 9:43]**. (B) is proclaimed, full force, by strings and winds **[T2/i8, 10:08]**, and surges ahead like some primeval lava flow, breaking the triple-forte sound barrier (*fff*) to arrive at Mach 4 (*ffff*) **[T2/i8, 10:49]**.

Once more the Fate motive sounds its warning signal **[T2/i9, 11:15]**; once more it quickly vanishes, leaving a tangle of vapor trails. All is serenity once again **[T2/i10, 12:01]**; over the winds' quiet, steady throbbing in triplets, the strings propose a kindly, gentle version of (B), gradually dying out **[T2/i10, 13:20]**, with the clarinets in the last two bars pronouncing a benediction.

Third movement: **Valse,** *Allegro moderato*

> *To know Tchaikovsky at all is to know his mastery of the waltz: the sumptuous examples in the major ballet scores, the* Serenade for

> Strings—*and this ravishing, shadowy symphonic treatment. The*
> *introduction of a dance movement to lighten the progression of serious*
> *thinking in the symphony goes back at least as far as Haydn's minuets.*
> *Beethoven (known as a lousy dancer) quickened the pace to a scherzo*
> *(Italian for "joke"), sometimes more sardonic than witty. Antonín*
> *Dvorák's symphonies usually included one movement in the measure*
> *of the furiant, a popular Bohemian dance with irregular, stomping*
> *accents. Thus, Tchaikovsky's evocation of the waltz as a relief from the*
> *fate-driven seriousness of the first two movements of the* Fifth
> Symphony, *was hardly unprecedented.*

The elegant waltz [theme (A), or, according to Dr. Spaeth, "waltz a little daily, keep the rhythm clear..."] begins immediately in the first violins **[T3/i1, 0:00]**, gently punctuated by pizzicatos in the lower strings
(on the second beat) and shafts of subdued light from bassoons and
horns (on the third). This first phrase is repeated with more resonance
[T3/i1, 0:17] by the first and second violins, with winds, horns, and
lower strings in a more flowing accompaniment that also provides a
light wash of dissonant harmonies. Oboe and bassoon take up the second part of the tune **[T3/i1, 0:28]**, and pass it on to the clarinets
[T3/i1, 0:39]. (Note here the special piquancy in the accompaniment
achieved by muting the horns.) The first part returns once more, in the
almost-full orchestra **[T3/i1, 1:02]**; then—a magical touch—the solo
bassoon proposes a sort of pendant, call it (B), to the main melody,
[T3/i2, 1:19], and this is taken up by flutes, clarinets and both bassoons.

You will surely notice the special care with which Tchaikovsky "shades"
his scoring. It's not that two flutes or clarinets or bassoons make a
louder noise than one of each; it's more that a solo wind makes a
different, more personal kind of sound than does two or three. And so
Tchaikovsky is careful to specify whether he wants one solo instrument
or more in his wind scoring all the way along. This theme (B) we've
just heard was introduced by the first of the two bassoons, but repeated
by both bassoons. Back at 0:27, the second part of the tune was
proposed by single oboe and bassoon, but taken up at 0:40 by two
clarinets. Think back to the famous horn passage at the start of the
slow movement; its poignancy, its intensely personal expression, is
surely the result of its being scored for a solo player; the strange, other-
worldly sounds at 0:40 in the waltz come from all four horn players,
with their instruments muted.

A prancing, skittering theme runs through the strings **[T3/i3, 1:41]**
to introduce a central contrasting section; it could be a dance for the
snowflakes in the as-yet-unwritten *Nutcracker*. The tune flits through
the string section in a lively game of question-and-answer. It then
passes to the flutes and piccolo **[T3/i3, 2:10]**, then through the entire
wind section, while the strings weave a slower countermelody
through all this buzzing activity.

Theme (A) returns **[T3/i4, 3:14]** in the oboes, while the strings
take their own sweet time about abandoning their merriment. Solo
oboe and bassoon take up the second strain as before, again with the
muted horns **[T3/i4, 3:36=0:28]**. The solo bassoon regains its acces-
sory theme **[T3/i5, 4:27=1:19]**. A closing section is initiated as the

strings take up a new variant of (A) **[T3/i6, 4:50]**, answered with lit-
tle giggles from clarinets and bassoons; this sequence repeats **[T3/i6, 5:13]**. Just as you might think the dancers are about to leave, the clarinets and bassoons sound their note of warning, a waltz-time variant
of the Fate theme (X1+X2) **[T3/i6, 5:29]**. The intrusion is short-
lived, however; the waltz fades out on its own **[T3/i6, 5:51]**, and six
brusque chords from the full orchestra end it.

Finale: ***Andante maestoso* leading to *Allegro vivace***
                           (Slow and majestic, fast and lively)

The operative word here is "maestoso" and, indeed, the Fate
motif—aka (X), aka "Glory to God in the highest"—returns now in
full majesty, its morose E minor now transformed to a brilliant E
major. (The note "E" is the highest open string on the violin; composers since Bach have chosen this key for music that will call for
maximum brilliance in the high range. Examples: Bach's *Partita No.
3* for solo violin; Mendelssohn's *Violin Concerto;* the preludes to Acts
I and III of Verdi's *La traviata*, all of which take the violin or violins
up into the stratosphere.) The strings proclaim the tune in a fairly low
register at the start, however **[T4/i1, 0:00]**; there will be plenty of time
to scale the heights. The brass take up the born-again theme over a
pizzicato accompaniment **[T4/i1, 0:46]**, leading to a solemn cadence.
Now the woodwinds take on the theme **[T4/i1, 1:11]** over a flowing
triplet accompaniment. The brass seem impatient to move on, how-

ever, and sound a summons derived from the Fate theme **[T4/i1, 1:54]**. The sense of urgency grows, with the growl of the timpani **[T4/i1, 2:21]** adding to the tension and eventually pushing the speed up to *Allegro vivace*, the tempo of the main part of the movement.

> *At the start, this movement fostered the most trouble with critics, the public, and musicians. Johannes Brahms, who attended rehearsals in Hamburg, had high praise for everything in the symphony except the last movement. The sentiment was widely shared. "In the finale," wrote a Boston critic at the first performance there, in 1892, "we have all the untamed fury of the Cossack, whetting itself for deeds of atrocity...The furious peroration sounds like nothing so much as a horde of demons struggling in a torrent of brandy, the music growing drunker and drunker. Pandemonium, delirium tremens, raving, and above all, noise worse confounded!"*

> *The movement is long, and does thrash a bit; yet by the time it achieves its apotheosis, a great performance should make the audience want to stand up, wave flags, and perhaps release flocks of white doves. Some conductors have tried to institute cuts; there are recordings by Willem Mengelberg and Artur Rodzinski, perhaps by others as well, that lop off a large chunk midway in the movement (from about 5:14 to 7:46 on the Dutoit recording). This does nothing but destroy the logic in the shape of the movement.*

Exposition

In E minor, (A) is a furious whirlwind of sound **[T4/i2, 2:55]**; the strings start it, the woodwinds soon join in and the brass and timpani punctuate the cadence. A transitional theme, (B) **[T4/i3, 3:16]**, strikes a gentler, more flowing tone over a pulsating accompaniment in the second violins and violas. A second transitional, (C) **[T4/i4, 3:31]**, in the strings with the winds taking up the pulsations, speeds the action forward; a mighty roll on the timpani subsides to a monotonous throbbing: a moment of suspense. The second theme, (D), is in D major, a key fairly remote from E minor (although the first movement followed the same key-scheme); the music takes on a lyrical flow, stated first by the winds **[T4/i5, 3:58]** over sustained notes in the brass and a tricky, bristling string figuration (six notes to the bar in the upper strings versus four to the bar in the cellos and basses). The consequent phrase of (D) is an upside-down version of the theme as it was first heard **[T4/i5, 4:17]**. This leads to a brassy declaration of (X), accompanied by swirling clouds of string tone in the even more remote key of C major **[T4/i6, 4:39]**, and the music moves without a break into the development section.

Development

As in the first movement, the development is quite short, less than two minutes out of a total of thirteen-and-a-half. It begins **[T4/i7, 5:14]** with a variation on (A), with the lowest brass sounding a series of oddly dissonant sustained notes, like foghorns through the mist **[T4/i7, 5:23]**. (D) shows up in its upside-down configuration **[T4/i8, 5:36]** and echoes through the orchestra in a moment of clear, if complex, counterpoint; but this begins to die down **[T4/i8, 6:04]** and starts a long decline toward a moment of suspenseful near-silence.

Recapitulation

Bang! The stillness is broken as the full orchestra reenters with a tense variant of (A) **[T4/i9, 6:34]** that gradually assumes the shape it had at the start of the exposition. For a time, the sequence of events follows the pattern of the exposition, but with a different order of key changes: transitional themes (B) **[T4/i10, 6:59=3:16]** and (C) **[T4/i11, 7:13=3:58]**. The second theme, (D), returns in the key of F-sharp minor **[T4/i12, 7:46=3:58]**. Now the music begins to surge forward as if possessed. The Fate motive returns **[T4/i13, 8:31=4:39]**; the music speeds up, with the rhythm of (X) supplying the momentum **[T4/i13, 8:44]** and leading to a huge, emphatic catching of the breath **[T4/i13, 8:57]**—a cadence that some in the audience mistake for the symphony's end, and sometimes triggers applause.

Coda

The Fate theme strides forth in its ultimate glory, over a surging, throbbing triplet figuration in the winds. The key is definitively E major **[T4/i14, 9:20]**. The music gets grander and grander; the trumpets pick up (X) **[T4/i15, 10:10]** and blast it heavenward—they should really be standing at this point, and so should the audience.

The pace quickens; the transition (B) is accorded a working-over [T4/i16, 10:51]. But the last word, surprisingly, belongs to the actual first theme of the first movement (A), (Dr. Spaeth's "then rally around in the cause of mankind...") [T4/i17, 11:24], tying the entire symphony together ever more firmly, and bringing the forty-six minutes of music, by turns stirring, agonizing, and heartwarming, to a stunning close.

Romeo and Juliet, Fantasy Overture after Shakespeare

Scoring: *two flutes and piccolo, two oboes and English horn, two clarinets, bassoons and trumpets, four horns, three trombones and tuba; timpani, bass drum and cymbals, harp and strings. First version, completed in 1869, first performance 16 March 1870, Moscow; second version, completed in 1870, first performance 17 February 1872, St. Petersburg; third version, completed in 1880, first performance 1 May 1886, Tbilisi.*

"Like all young Russia, Tchaikovsky is naturally a 'musician of the future.' In his overture *Romeo and Juliet* there steams cold, glistening smoke, there rages heated noise. As an illustration of a Verona family feud, the Allegro sounds decidedly too Russian; one actually hears the blows of the knout falling in heavy strokes unconnected with any bar division. In St. Petersburg they probably say

it more poetically: 'Thus pounds Fate on the bass drum.'
Eight softening bars tell us unambiguously that we
approach a love scene. But this motive built on the alternation of two dissonant chords sounds rather like
scratching on a glass plate with a sharp knife. Like a cold
snakeskin this love-bliss runs down the spine."

—Critic Eduard Hanslick,
the *Vienne Neue freie Presse,* 30 November 1876

Mily Balakirev, a largely self-taught composer from Nizhni-
Novgorod, settled in St. Petersburg in 1855 and immediately established himself as the paterfamilias of a group of similarly untrained
but enthusiastic composers. They dubbed themselves "The Russian
Five" and declared as their aim the purging of Russian music of outside (i.e., German and Italian) influences, to create a native, folk-
based musical language. Modest Mussorgsky (army ensign and res-
olute drunkard), Aleksandr Borodin (chemist), César Cui (army
engineer), and Nicolay Rimsky-Korsakov (naval cadet) pooled their
philosophies with those of Balakirev (the only full-time para-profes-
sional in the bunch) toward this nationalistic end, with some success.
Tchaikovsky resisted the temptation to join the group, but his rela-
tions with the Five weren't all that bad. We can thank the benign
counsel of Balakirev in the shaping of Tchaikovsky's first masterpiece,
an "overture-fantasy" inspired by Shakespeare's *Romeo and Juliet.*

In 1868, Tchaikovsky composed a symphonic poem called
Fatum (our old friend Fate once again). It was dedicated to Balakirev,

who conducted the first St. Petersburg performance. He then communicated to Tchaikovsky his strong reservations about the piece, whereupon Tchaikovsky destroyed it. (It was reconstructed in 1896, three years after Tchaikovsky's death: a sprawling, messy piece with some pretty tunes.) Tchaikovsky accepted Balakirev's criticisms and promised to write something better for him in the near future. That turned out to be the orchestral tone poem inspired by Shakespeare's tragedy. Balakirev kept watch over Tchaikovsky's shoulder throughout the shaping of the work, and intensified his interference after a first version (conducted by Nikolay Rubinstein in 1870) made the work's flaws abundantly clear. It was Balakirev who suggested the opening hymn-like chorale, found the first version of the love theme "a bit overripe," and who outlined a wholesale reordering of the orchestration and the arrangement of keys. For the first and last time in his life, Tchaikovsky had acquiesced to a near-total rewrite of a work that had already cost him considerable effort. But his submission paid off.

As a composer on his own, Mily Balakirev ranks as somewhat below first-class. As a tinkerer with others' music, though, he proved himself proficient beyond challenge. (The Five developed a tradition of tinkering, in fact, as witness Rimsky-Korsakov's "corrections" imposed on Mussorgsky's *Boris Godunov*.) The new and improved *Romeo and Juliet* had an acclaimed premiere in St. Petersburg in 1872. On his own, Tchaikovsky made some more adjustments; the ultimate new and further improved *Romeo,* completed in 1880, had its first performance in Tbilisi in 1886. Don't be misled by the term "overture," by the way; there is no *Romeo and Juliet* opera by Tchaikovsky, with an overture leading into further action. "Overture" can also refer to an independent orchestral piece, as in the *Academic Festival* and *Tragic Overtures* by Brahms or Wagner's *Faust Overture.* The idea of a *Romeo* opera may, indeed, have occurred to Tchaikovsky somewhere along the way, however. He did sketch a duet for soprano and tenor, using themes from the *Overture,* with Shakespeare's words translated by Aleksandr Sokolovsky, but left it incomplete. It was found among his papers after his death, and completed by Sergey Taneyev—a pretty morsel for the collector who must have everything.

The outline for the piece could not be simpler; it is, in fact, a shapely compression of the action of the play, with the major characters and situations clearly identified at the start and throughout the story. It is a pictorial tone poem far simpler in outline than any of Franz Liszt's speculative and spiritual works. It succeeds owing to the beauty of its story and the beauty of Tchaikovsky's capturing of it in his fragrant and stirring music.

> *It is easy to attach titles to the themes of this work; they obviously cling to the characters in Shakespeare's tragedy and appear in pretty much the same chronological order of events in the play. That said, however, there is no way that the one work could stand in for the other; Tchaikovsky's* Overture *blends the outline of the play with a totally symphonic sense of structure. The two battle scenes relate to one another as the exposition and development of a symphonic movement;*

*the second occurrence of the Love theme relates to the first occurrence
in much the same way as the triumphant stride of the Fate theme in
the last movement of the* Fifth Symphony *relates to the shape of that
theme at the start of the first movement. What is remarkable about*
Romeo and Juliet—*one of its many remarkable aspects, that is—is
Tchaikovsky's genius in shading the main themes of the work to mirror
the drama: the change in Romeo's theme from his first tentative
declaration of love to the ardent later promises, to the deep sadness that
the theme takes on near the end, to the lush harmonic transformation
of the Romeo theme in the final bars. For all its popularity, this is a
deep and subtle work, and it's not surprising that its creation caused
Tchaikovsky so much pain over so long a time.*

Clarinets and bassoons sound the solemn harmonies of the theme
[T5/i1, 0:00] that will represent Friar Laurence (although one musicologist has suggested that the theme really stands for "the burden of
fate"). The chords have a chorale-like flavor, and also prophecy the
similar sounds at the start of the second movement of Tchaikovsky's
Fifth Symphony (and, for that matter, the "1812" Overture). The
strings make their first entry **[T5/i1, 0:34]** in a slow contrapuntal passage that could be the start of a fifteenth-century liturgical composition (except that the sighing dissonances are pure Russian-roman-
tic). The sounds are mysterious; the flutes have a melodic line that
rises in a slow crescendo **[T5/i1, 1:10]**. The harp adds a sequence of
mournful chords **[T5/i2, 1:33]**. The pizzicato strings set up a nervous
scurrying **[T5/i3, 2:10]** as the winds repeat the Friar Laurence theme

with greater urgency **[T5/i3, 2:16]**; the whole opening sequence, in fact, seems to be repeating but on a higher level of nervousness. Something's afoot, we sense.

The liturgical/contrapuntal passage is repeated **[T5/i3, 2:49=0:34]** and moves ahead to a reprise of the sorrowful harp chords **[T5/i3, 3:46=1:33]**. Over a menacing roll of the timpani that gradually grows louder, the liturgical counterpoint is heard again **[T5/i4, 4:20]**, increasing in speed and intensity and reaching what sounds like a cadence **[T5/i4, 4:58]**. But no—it starts up again—then breaks off. A moment of suspense **[T5/i4, 5:29]**: mysterious chords sound in winds and strings in alternation. Suddenly...

Bang! The Battle theme sounds its challenge: brusque, jagged, full of stops and starts, punctuated with bursts of white light from the piccolo **[T5/i5, 5:43]**. Capulets and Montagues mix it up in the streets of fair Verona. The theme resounds again **[T5/i5, 6:09]**, this time with echoing answers in the low strings to thicken the sounds of strife. The shrillness of combined piccolo and flute hurls challenges at the strings and they respond **[T5/i5, 6:24]**. The strings set up a furious momentum, as winds and brass punctuate with brusque chords at irregular time intervals **[T5/i5, 6:37]**. The battle music breaks forth once again in full force **[T5/i5, 6:50]**, but a series of insistent chords from the brass slow the momentum at last **[T5/i5, 7:10]**. The activity subsides; short echoes of the preceding furor die out in the orchestra. We have come to Juliet's balcony.

A sound not heard before—the dusky, reedy voice of the solo English horn—sounds the music best known as the Love theme **[T5/i6, 7:51]**, surrounded by a halo of soft sound from muted violas and quiet chords from the horns. Actually, this is Romeo's love theme, ardent and rhapsodic. Juliet's answering love theme **[T5/i6, 8:10]** is sung by the muted violins, divided into four parts, playing in wavering, supple harmonies. The lovers touch, and so do their themes: Romeo's ever more declamatory in high winds **[T5/i6, 8:51]**, Juliet's in the silken tones of muted violins. Slowly, the music increases in volume and intensity; the poignant beauty becomes almost unbearable **[T5/i6, 9:34]**, until the final "sweet sorrow" of parting in a long fadeout over harmonious harps **[T5/i7, 9:51]** loses the idyll to cruel daylight. Only one other composer has ever translated the melancholic ecstasy of this Shakespearean moment into music that can stand beside Tchaikovsky's: Hector Berlioz, at this same moment in his long *Roméo et Juliette* Symphony. Comparing the two will give you an unmatchable hour of extraordinary music.

The dream ends; it is daylight in Verona, and the bitter enmity of warring families bears more poisoned fruit. The Battle theme breaks out once again **[T5/i8, 10:51]** in a slightly altered but recognizable variant. The Friar Laurence theme sounds from inside the rush of strings and brass **[T5/i8, 11:03]**. Bits of the theme swirl around and combine with one another; the air is heavy with menace. Now the battle gains in intensity **[T5/i9, 12:32]**, with trumpets yelling out the Laurence theme as if invoking Heaven's intercession—but they are not heeded. The Battle theme returns once more in its original shape [T5/i9, 13:08=5:43], but with punctuation from cymbal and bass drum and further intensification from the roar of trombones and tuba.

The music subsides [T5/i10, 13:33]; for a few moments Juliet's love theme hangs suspended in the winds, while echoes of the battle fade out in the violins. But the moment of quietude vanishes; against a persistent throb in the winds and a mass of enveloping sound in the brass and timpani, the strings scream out Romeo's theme [T5/i11, 14:12]. The orchestra seems to be playing on tiptoes, so urgent is the sound. A climactic full statement of both Romeo's and Juliet's love themes sounded simultaneously [T5/i11, 14:54] seems to be pushing relentlessly toward another climax (perhaps in more ways than one).

That happens [T5/i12, 15:44]. The Love themes fade away as the echoes of battle are heard one last time [T5/i12, 15:53]. The strings continue their rushing about, but a gradual clearing seems to be taking place [T5/i12, 16:09]. Now the stage has emptied; shadows close in [T5/i12, 16:46].

As the timpani set up a funereal throbbing, over a sustained note in the low brass, the violins intone a mournful harmonization of a fragment of Romeo's theme [T5/i13, 17:19]. The winds and horns present another fragment, this time of the Friar Laurence theme as heard in the Prologue; this blends into a fragment of Juliet's theme [T5/i13, 18:06]. And over the familiar melancholy of chords from the harp, Romeo's theme sounds once more **[T5/i14, 19:17]**, in harmonies even more mournful than any previously heard. Yet the final brusque chords, in irregular, offbeat accents similar to what we heard in the first battle scene (6:37), tell us that the fight goes on.

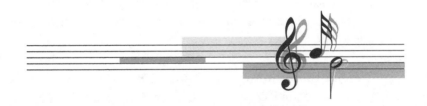

Basic Tchaikovsky
The Essential Recordings

1 ***Symphony No. 5 in E minor, Opus 64.*** Charles Dutoit conducting the Montreal Symphony Orchestra. London 425503-2. Romeo and Juliet Fantasy Overture. London 430 507-2.

See the Play by Play chapter for a detailed journey through these works.

2 ***Piano Concerto No. 1 in B flat minor, Opus 23 (*** with ***Chopin: Piano Concerto No. 2 in F minor, Opus 21).*** Vladimir Ashkenazy, pianist, with Lorin Maazel conducting the London Symphony Orchestra. London 417 750-2.

No other repertory work this popular holds onto its secrets so tenaciously. A gorgeously colored façade, those first few minutes, fronts a haunted house full of dark corners. Nikolay Rubinstein, Tchaikovsky's usually benevolent mentor, savaged the work at first hearing; Hans von Bülow, the virtuoso who first played the concerto in public (in Boston!) called it Tchaikovsky's "fullest" work to date. Compared to the sweet elegance of Chopin's *F-minor Concerto*, a far more typical example of the Romantic virtuosic work, the daring in Tchaikovsky's concerto continues to amaze. From its thunderous opening to the gossamer of much of the second movement, its stylistic sweep is broad and secure.

TRACKS 1-3:

Piano Concerto No. 1 in B flat minor

Track 1:

Allegro non troppo e molto maestoso

0:00	Introduction: horn solo (B flat minor)
0:14	First theme: strings, piano chords (D flat major)
0:57	First theme repeat: piano, pizzicato strings (D flat major)
1:24	Cadenza bridge
2:28	First theme repeat: tutti (D flat major)
3:08	Bridge leading to F minor
4:11	F major orchestra chords
4:40	Second theme: piano (B flat minor)
5:06	Second theme developed
5:50	Variation on second theme: piano
6:06	Bridge to lyrical third theme
6:14	Lyrical third theme (A flat major): winds, then piano
7:03	Theme 3A for strings, derived from third theme
7:33	Third theme: piano
8:25	Cadenza bridge
9:05	Theme 3A: strings, winds
9:49	Orchestral development of theme 3A
11:00	Extended piano cadenza
12:17	Canonic development
12:54	Additional development
13:48	Recapitulation of second theme: piano
14:17	Recapitulation of lyrical third

theme: oboe (B flat major)

15:00 Recapitulation of third theme: clarinet (B flat major)

15:15 Beginning of development leading to finale

16:14 Extended piano cadenza based on third and 3A themes

19:30 Theme 3A: tutti orchestra (B flat major)

20:25 Coda

Andantino semplice

0:00 Bed of pizzicato string chords (D flat major)

0:13 First theme: flute (D flat major)

0:39 First theme: piano over lyrical string bed

1:06 Second theme: winds/strings (F major)

1:20 Theme 2A: winds/strings (D major)

1:46 Development, using first theme head: winds

2:13 Recapitulation of first theme: cello solo (D flat major)

2:39 First theme: oboe (D flat major)

3:13 Developmental bridge

(scherzo): piano (central section)

3:34 Third theme: strings (D flat major)

4:08 Bridge (scherzo material): piano

4:28 Cadenza bridge

5:04 Recapitulation of first theme: piano over lyrical string bed

5:33 First theme: oboe variation

6:00 Coda (first theme head): piano, flute, strings

Allegro con fuoco

0:00 Orchestral introduction

0:05 First theme: piano (B flat minor)

0:31 Repeat of first theme: piano

0:40 Second theme (boisterous): orchestra (G flat major)

0:50 Bridge

1:04 Third theme (lyrical): strings, piano (D flat major)

1:45 First theme: piano with variations (B flat minor)

1:59 First theme development

2:21 Second theme: orchestra (A flat major)

2:43 Third theme: strings, piano (E flat major)

3:15 First theme: piano

3:42 Development

4:14 Slower tempo: first theme bridge to finale (B flat major)

4:25 Third theme bridge: strings

4:56 Brief piano cadenza

5:12 Majestic third theme: tutti (B flat major)

5:51 Coda: first theme (B flat major)

TRACKS 4-6:

Chopin: Piano Concerto No. 2 in F minor

Track 4:

Maestoso

0:00 First theme: orchestra (F minor)

1:16 Second theme: winds (A flat major)

2:34 First theme: piano (F minor)

4:36 Second theme: piano (A flat major)

5:58 Developmental bridge, third material: piano/orchestra

7:01 Orchestral tutti (C minor): development

7:53 First theme development: piano, wind solos (A flat major)

8:54 Dramatic development of first theme: piano and orchestra

9:58 Orchestral climax in return to tonic key

10:20 Recapitulation of first theme: piano (F minor)

10:33 Recapitulation of second theme: piano (A flat major)

11:53 Recapitulation of developmental third material: tutti

12:50 Measured piano cadenza

13:09 Orchestral climax in F minor; recapitulation of first theme

Track 5:

Larghetto

0:00 Orchestral introduction

0:32 Piano entrance

0:42 First theme (lyrical): piano (A flat major)

1:31 First theme extension (A flat major)

2:31 Repeat of first theme with variation: modulation to A flat minor

4:13 Rhapsodic cadenza-like central
section: piano, trem. strings

6:15 Slow piano cadenza bridge

6:30 Recapitulation of first theme
with variation (A flat major)

7:24 First theme extension:
piano/bassoon over strings

8:17 Orchestral coda (as
introduction)

8:47 Closing piano arpeggio

minor)

2:06 Second theme (scherzando):
piano (A flat major)

4:08 Development of second theme

5:13 Return to first theme (F minor)

5:40 Development bridge using first
theme material

6:30 F major arrival: horn call

6:37 New theme based on first
theme (F major)

7:49 Coda: piano: tutti

Track 6:

Allegro vivace (rondo finale)

0:00 First theme, piano: tutti (F
minor)

0:56 Repeat of first theme: piano (F

3 *Symphony No. 4 in F minor* and *Overture 1812 in E flat, Opus 49.* Christoph von Dohnanyi conducting the Cleveland Orchestra. London 425 792-2.

The *Fourth*, which Tchaikovsky always described to Madame von Meck as "our" symphony, is the first of many late works built in the shadow of threatening fate. The opening stentorian fanfares sound the menace, and return at the end to break off the dizzying gaiety of the finale. The orchestration in the work is a continual marvel, with the pizzicato strings in the scherzo recalling some of Tchaikovsky's ballet scores. The thrice-familiar "1812" Overture celebrates the victory of the Russians over the Napoleonic invaders, and does so once again with folk melodies: the songs of the French and Russians, with the Russian hymn triumphant amidst cannon fire at the end.

TRACKS 1-4:

Symphony No. 4 in F minor, Op. 36

Track 1:

Andante sostenuto/Moderato con anima

0:00	Andante sostenuto: introduction
1:03	Theme 1, complete
1:28	Moderato con anima: theme 1, part I
2:38	Transition to theme 1, part II
3:24	Theme 1, part II
4:53	Transition; closing section; transition to moderato assai
5:30	Moderato assai, quasi andante: theme 2, part I
6:34	Theme 2, part II (ben sostenuto il tempo precedente); development drawing from theme 1
7:47	Moderato con anima (tempo del comincio); climax;

transition to recapitulation of introduction

9:04 Recapitulation: introduction with development

9:24 Further development

11:30 Development to climax with material from introduction

13:06 Moderato assai, quasi andante: recapitulation of theme 2, part I, with development

14:17 Recapitulation: theme 2, part II, with development (ben sostenuto il tempo precedente)

15:29 Allegro con anima: development with material from theme 1 and introduction

16:06 Recapitulation: introduction with development from theme 1; extension; transition to più mosso

17:05 Molto più mosso: closing section

Track 2:

Andantino in modo di canzona

0:00 Theme 1, part I: oboe solo

0:39 Theme 1, part I: cello solo; short development; transition

to theme 1, part II

1:17 Theme 1, part II

1:56 Theme 1, part II; short development; transition to recapitulation of theme 1, part I

2:15 Recapitulation: theme 1, parts I and II

2:48 Recapitulation: theme 1, part II; closing section; transition to più mosso

3:40 Più mosso: theme 2 with development

4:32 Theme 2; climax; transition to recapitulation of theme 1, part I

5:24 Recapitulation: theme 1, part I: andantino; development

5:59 Recapitulation: theme 1, part II, with development

6:24 Extension: development of material from theme 1

7:44 Recapitulation: theme 1, part I: bassoon solo; closing section

Scherzo: pizzicato ostinato/allegro

0:00 Theme 1, part I: strings (pizzicato)

0:35 Theme 1, part II

0:57 Recapitulation: theme 1, part I

1:07 Extension and transition to meno mosso

1:43 Meno mosso: theme 2, part I: winds

2:21 Scherzo: theme 2, part II: brass

2:33 Theme 2, parts I and II, with development and transition to recapitulation of theme 1, part I

2:58 Recapitulation: theme 1, part I

3:34 Recapitulation: theme 1, part II

3:55 Recapitulation: theme 1, part I

4:05 Extension and transition to development

4:37 Development: winds and strings; climax

5:15 Recapitulation: theme 2, part II; closing

Finale: Allegro con fuoco

0:00 Introduction

0:43 Theme 1

1:10 Extension and climax

1:31 Theme 2 with development

2:34 Development of theme 2 as trasnition to recapitulation of introduction

2:55 Recapitulation: introduction

3:04 Recapitulation: theme 1

3:31 Extension and climax

3:52 Recapitulation: theme 2 with development

5:15 Recapitulation: introduction from movement 1 (track 1): andante sostenuto

6:33 Allegro con fuoco: transition back to introduction, movement 4

7:07 Recapitulation: introduction

7:13 Recapitulation: theme 1 with development

7:25 Development: theme 1 as closing section

TRACK 5:

1812 Overture

0:00 Largo: hymn

2:01 Theme of the coming battle (foreboding)

3:48 Andante: Russian army anthem: "God Save the Czar"

4:43 Allegro giusto: the battle

5:26 The "Marseillaise" (used throughout from here on)

6:45 Slower: romance (theme of the home and earth)

8:15 Russian peasant dance

8:53 Recapitulation of battle theme and "Marseillaise"

10:30 Slower: recapitulation of romance

11:13 Recapitulation: Russian peasant dance

11:30 Cavalry charge, drawn from battle theme and "Marseillaise"; climax

12:57 Recapitulation: hymn: largo; with "bells of Moscow"

14:01 Allegro vivace: closing section

4 *Symphony No. 6 in B minor, "Pathétique," Opus 74* and *Suite from "The Nutcracker," Opus 71.* Simeon Bychkov conducting the Berlin Philharmonic Orchestra. Philips 434 150-2.

The work failed with the public its first time out; even from Tchaikovsky's pen, this was an uncommonly bitter message. The wild gaiety of its third movement, quenched by the mighty lamentation that begins the fourth is one of the most brutal events in the entire realm of symphonic music. The symphony was first performed on 28 November 1893; a week later Tchaikovsky was dead. Had he, in fact, composed his own requiem in those last pages, with the single note on the gong a summons from another world? (One refutation lies in the enchanting, light-hearted dances from "The Nutcracker," also from Tchaikovsky's last months on earth. Is this really the work of a man obsessed with death?) The matter is still being argued, but the place of the Sixth Symphony among the world's imperishable masterworks is now beyond argument.

TRACKS 1-4:

Symphony No. 6 in B minor, Op. 74

Track 1:

Adagio/Allegro non troppo

0:00 Adagio: introduction

2:25 Allegro non troppo: theme 1, part I

3:14 Theme 1, part II

4:04 Transition to theme 2

5:05 Theme 2, part I

6:11 Theme 2, part II: development; extension; climax

7:39 Theme 2, parts I and II: recapitulation

8:39 Moderato assai: transition

9:39 Adagio mosso: introduction to development

10:33 Allegro vivo: development of theme 1

12:22 Transition to climax

13:45 Climax

15:09 Andante come prima: development of theme 2

16:11 Transition

17:55 Andante: closing section

Track 2:
Allegro con grazia

0:00 Theme 1

0:37 Theme 1: repeat

1:11 Theme 2

1:46 Recapitulation: theme 1, with development and extension

2:40 Theme 3, part I: trio

3:03 Theme 3, part I: repeat

3:26 Theme 3, part II

3:49 Theme 3, part II: repeat

4:12 Recapitulation: theme 3, part I

4:35 Transition to recapitulation, theme 1

5:19 Recapitulation: theme 1, with development

5:55 Recapitulation: theme 2, with development

6:29 Recapitulation: theme 1, with development

6:56 Extension and transition to closing section

7:23 Closing section

Track 3:
Allegro molto vivace

0:00 Theme 1

0:27 Theme 1 with development

0:53 Development and transition

1:27 Closing section

1:39 Further development and transition to theme 2

2:18 Theme 2

2:41 Recapitulation: theme 1 with development

4:02 Transition; development; extension

4:40 Transition to climax

5:07 Climax; transition to recapitulation of theme 2

6:06 Recapitulation: theme 2 with development

6:36 Recapitulation: theme 1, with extension and climax

7:39 Closing section

Track 4:

Adagio lamentoso/Andante

0:00 Adagio lamentoso: theme 1

1:20 Development: theme 1

2:55 Andante: theme 2

3:37 Development: theme 2, with extension and climax

5:18 Transition to recapitulation of theme 1

5:48 Recapitulation: theme 1 with development (andante non tanto)

7:04 Recapitulation: theme 1 with further development

7:25 Further development and climax

8:41 Transition to closing section

9:28 Closing section

TRACKS 5-12:

Nutcracker Suite, Op. 71

Track 5:

Miniature overture
Allegro giusto

0:00 Theme 1

0:44 Theme 2

1:08 Transition to closing section

1:17 Closing section

1:28 Recapitulation: theme 1 with development

2:11 Recapitulation: theme 2 with development

2:35 Transition to closing section

2:44 Closing section

Tracks 6-12:

Characteristic Dances

Track 6:

Marche
Tempo di marcia viva

0:00 Theme 1, part I

0:27 Theme 1, part II

0:39 Recapitulation: theme 1, part I

1:05 Theme 2

1:18 Recapitulation: theme 1, part I, with development

1:45 Recapitulation: theme 1, part II, with development

1:57 Recapitulation: theme 1, part I, with development and ending

5 *Violin Concerto in D, Opus 35 (*with *Sibelius: Violin Concerto in D minor, Opus 47).* Viktoria Mullova, violin, with Seiji Ozawa conducting the Boston Symphony Orchestra. Philips 416 821-2.

Like the *First Piano Concerto,* the *Violin Concerto* was denounced by its original dedicatee (Leopold Auer, the famous virtuoso and teacher) as "unplayable." (That epithet has also been lavished on the Sibelius Violin Concerto, a piece clearly inspired by Tchaikovsky's. It hasn't injured the fame of either work.) If there is such a thing as a "pure" Russian composition, it might be this concerto, with its robust melodic energy of the first movement, the winsome melancholy of the second, and the dizzying dances of the finale.

TRACKS 1-3:

Violin Concerto in D, Op. 35

Track 1:
Allegro moderato

0:00 Orchestral introduction (D major)

0:52 Violin entrance: brief cadenza

1:10 First theme: violin (D major)

2:16 Theme 1A: violin (D major)

2:42 Theme 1A: orchestra (F major; A major)

3:15 Second theme (lyrical) in dominant: violin (A major)

4:06 Second theme: variation and development

5:28 Allegro theme 2A (derived from second theme)

5:19 First theme return: orchestra tutti (A major)

6:52 Modulation and development

7:39 First theme, variation (C major)

8:50 First theme, original form: orchestra tutti (F major)

9:30 Arrival in dominant key: violin cadenza

12:20 Recapitulation of first theme: flute, violin (D major)

13:15 Theme 1A: violin (A major)

13:40 Theme 1A: orchestra

14:14 Recapitulation of second theme (lyrical): violin (D major)

14:58 Modulation and development of second theme

16:02 Recapitulation of theme 2A: dominant pedal point

16:35 Accelerando bridge to coda, finale

16:55 Finale begins

17:32 False cadence on minor subdominant

17:39 Tutti arrival on tonic; coda at faster tempo

Track 2:
Canzonetta (Andante)

0,00 Orchestra introduction: winds

0:37 First theme (lyrical): extended violin solo (G minor)

1:48 First theme: winds

2:08 Second theme: violin (E flat major)

3:05 Modulation back to tonic key

3:30 Recapitulation of first theme (variations with winds): violin (G minor)

4:58 Introductory material for winds

on dominant (D major)

5:21 Antiphonal strings and winds: modulation to A major

Track 3:
Finale (Allegro vivacissimo)

0:00 Attaca: orchestra from previous movement: allegro (A major)

0:13 Violin cadenza (A major)

0:42 First theme: violin (D major)

1:28 Theme 1A: violin (B minor)

1:48 Second theme (pesante): violin (A major)

2:15 Second theme: faster with variations

2:41 Second theme transformed and slower in F minor

3:00 Second theme and development: violin (E major)

3:48 First theme recapitulation (D major)

4:26 First theme modulation and variation

5:07 Second theme (pesante): violin (G major)

5:32 Second theme: faster with variations

6:01 Second theme transformed,

slower (E minor)

6:26 Second theme and
development: violin (E minor)

7:26 Recapitulation of first theme:
violin (D major)

8:24 Dominant pedal point

8:42 Tonic arrival (D major); coda
based on first theme

TRACKS 4-6:

Sibelius: Violin Concerto in D Minor, Op. 47

Track 4:

Allegro moderato

0:00 First theme: violin (D minor)

1:12 First theme: variation,
interplay with orchestra

2:00 Violin cadenza

2:45 Orchestral interlude,
modulation to B flat major

4:12 Second theme: violin in sixths

5:10 Third theme (lyrical): violin

5:40 Orchestral interlude (B flat
minor)

7:26 Violin cadenza, orchestral
accompagnata

7:56 Violin cadenza, solo

9:51 Recapitulation of first theme:
bassoon/violin (G minor)

11:00 Return to D minor

11:42 Developmental interlude:
orchestra; modulation to B
major

12:49 Oboe/cello duet (B major)

13:13 Violin solo re-enters

13:29 Second theme, violin in sixths
(D major, D minor)

14:23 Third theme (lyrical) (F Major -
D minor)

14:51 Virtuoso finale based on first
material (D minor)

15:40 Final statement of first theme

Track 5:

Adagio di molto

0:00 Introduction for winds:
extended cantilena

0:40 Accompanied violin solo,
adagio (B flat major)

3:00 Second theme: orchestral
interlude chromatically
developed

3:44 Violin response (doublestops)
to orchestra: leads to G minor

4:44 Recapitulation of first theme:

violin/orchestral tutti (B flat major)

5:35 Rising violin figure imitates bassi string pizzicato (opening)

7:38 Coda

Track 6:

Allegro, ma non tanto

0:00 First theme (allegro): violin solo (D major)

0:38 Theme 1A (derived from first theme): violin

1:19 Orchestral interlude

1:26 Second theme: orchestra (G minor)

1:55 Violin variations on second theme

2:34 Interlude (B flat major)

3:00 Development: violin over orchestra (f sharp minor)

3:39 Recapitulation of first theme: tutti (D major)

3:52 Recapitulation of first theme: violin (D major)

4:05 Restatement of theme 1A

4:55 Orchestral interlude

5:02 Restatement and variations of second theme: violin, orchestra (D minor)

6:09 Dominant pedal point, leading to last tonic arrival

6:53 Finale, dramatic D major arrival, tonic key pedal point

6 *Swan Lake, Opus 20.* Charles Dutoit conducting the Montreal Symphony Orchestra. London 436 212-2.

You need to check out the repertory of the Imperial Theater before *Swan Lake* (works by Leon Minkus, Léo Delibes, etc.) to realize what a step forward Tchaikovsky's first full-length ballet represented: a work of such strength and dramatic impact that it can be listened to in concert as well as in theater. Prepare for a shiver the first time the chilly B-minor theme heralds the flight of swans across the gray sky; prepare once again as that theme thunders forth, transformed to a major key, to bring down the curtain on this weird but stirring scenario.

DISC 1

Act I

Track 1:
No. 1

0:00 Introduction (moderato assai): theme 1

1:42 Allegro ma non troppo (introduction: theme 2)

2:07 Recapitulation of theme 1: attaca

2:50 Scene: allegro giusto: opening

3:21 Theme 1 (for No. 1)

4:11 Theme 2 (for No. 1)

4:51 Theme 1 recapitulation

Track 2:
No. 2: Scene: Valse (Tempo di valse)

0:00 Introduction

0:12 Theme 1

1:18 Theme 2

1:33 Theme 2, first development

1:47 Theme 2, second development (over harmony of theme 1)

2:21 Theme 2 (tutti)

2:35 Recapitulation: theme 1

3:36 Theme 3

4:06 Theme 3, first development

4:35 Recapitulation: theme 3

4:50 Theme 3, second development

5:20 Theme 3, third development

5:52 Recapitulation of theme 3; recapitulation theme 3, second development; transition

6:23 Recapitulation: theme 1

Track 3:

No. 3: Scene (Allegro moderato)

0:00 Theme 1

0:26 Theme 1, development

1:00 Transition

1:12 Recapitulation: theme 1

1:29 Theme 2

2:40 Recapitulation: theme 1 (variation)

3:13 Coda: fugue on theme 1 as transition to first theme of scene I

Track 4:

No. 4: Scene: Pas de trois

0:00 I: intrada: allegro: theme 1

0:39 Intrada: theme 2 (relative minor)

1:22 Intrada: recapitulation, theme 1

1:39 Closing

2:27 II: andante sostenuto: theme 1

2:49 Theme 2 (as upper layer of theme 1)

4:20 Recapitulation, theme 1, extended as coda

5:40 III: allegro simplice: theme 1

6:19 Theme 1: first development

6:44 Presto (stretto of theme 1)

7:00 IV: moderato: theme 1

7:28 Theme 1, second development

7:41 Transition to original theme 1 (from intrada I)

7:57 Recapitulation: theme 1

8:13 V: allegro: theme 1

8:29 Development: theme 2

8:45 Transition to original theme 1 (from intrada I)

8:57 Coda: theme 1

9:23 Coda: allegro vivace

9:49-11:06 Recapitulation of themes from each section

Track 5:

No. 5: Scene: Pas de deux

0:00 I: introduction: tempo di valse ma non troppo vivo, quasi moderato

0:12 Theme 1

0:59 Development: theme 1; coda, transition to andante

1:42 I: andante (violin cadenza): development of theme 1

3:09 Development, theme 1

5:34 Allegro: theme 1

6:07 Theme 2

6:29 Recapitulation: theme 1

6:49 Coda

7:12 III: tempo di valse: theme 1

7:48 Theme 2

8:11 Recapitulation: theme 1

8:46 IV: coda/allegro molto vivace: theme 1

9:11 First development: theme 1

9:29 Recapitulation: theme 1

9:42 Second development: theme 1

9:52 Recapitulation: first development

10:05 Recapitulation: theme 1

10:17 Closing

Track 6:

No. 6: Scene: Pas d'action

0:00 Andantino quasi moderato: theme 1

0:27 Development: theme 1 (upper layer)

0:53 Theme 2

1:18 Recapitulation: theme 1, with extension and further development

2:24 Beginning of stringendo

2:41 Allegro (stretto of theme 1)

Track 7:

No. 7: Scene: Sujet

0:00 Part I: clarinet solo

0:16 Part II: oboe solo

Track 8:

No. 8: Scene: Danse des coupes (Tempo di polacca)

0:00 Theme 1

0:42 Development: theme 1

0:59 Recapitulation: theme 1

1:33 Theme 2

1:59 Development: theme 2

2:35 Recapitulation: theme 2

2:47 Return through theme 2 to recapitulation: theme 1

3:12 Recapitulation: theme 1, plus new development

3:53 Return: development of theme 1

4:15 Return

4:35 Further development of theme 1 as coda

Track 9:
No. 9: Scene: Finale (Andante)

- 0:00 Theme 1
- 0:28 Theme 2
- 0:58 Recapitulation: theme 1 (tutti)
- 1:20 Development: theme 1 in major/closing

Act II

Track 10:
No. 10: Scene (Moderato)

- 0:00 Theme 1 (from andante/finale Act I)
- 0:27 Theme 2
- 0:56 Recapitulation: theme 1 (tutti)
- 1:19 Theme 2
- 1:43 Development: theme 2, used as extension
- 2:13 Stringendo: transition back to theme 1
- 2:24 Recapitulation: theme 1, with development

Track 11:
No. 11: Scene (Allegro moderato)

- 0:00 Theme 1A
- 0:29 Theme 1B
- 0:39 Recapitulation: Theme 1A with development and transition
- 1:26 Introduction to theme 2
- 1:49 Moderato: theme 2
- 2:09 Development: theme 2
- 2:29 Più mosso: transition to theme 3
- 3:10 Allegro vivo: theme 3
- 3:36 Development: theme 3
- 4:22 Theme 3 as coda and transition to l'istesso tempo
- 4:42 L'istesso tempo: development of theme 3 as coda

Track 12:
No. 12: Scene (Allegro)

- 0:00 Theme 1A
- 0:15 Theme 1B
- 0:26 Recapitulation: theme 1A
- 0:41 Recapitulation: theme 1B
- 0:52 Development
- 1:46 Theme 2A
- 2:02 Theme 2B
- 2:34 Moderato assai quasi andante/modified recapitulation of theme 2A

Track 13:
No. 13: Danses des cygnes

- 0:00 I: tempo di valse: theme 1

0:36 Theme 2A

0:53 Theme 2B

1:18 Recapitulation: theme 1

1:28 Theme 1

2:00 Closing

2:23 II: moderato assai: theme 1A

2:47 Theme 1B

3:05 Theme 1C

3:24 Recapitulation: theme 1A

3:43 Molto più mosso: development of theme 1 used for ending

4:13 III (IV): allegro moderato: theme 1A

*Section III was eliminated from this performance of the work

4:25 Theme 1B

4:34 Theme 2A

4:44 Theme 2B

4:54 Theme 2A

5:03 Theme 2B

5:13 Recapitulation: theme 1A

5:22 Recapitulation: theme 1B

5:31 Closing

5:45 IV: Pas d'action: introduction

6:15 Harp cadenza

6:57 Andante non troppo: theme 1 (harp and violin solo)

7:31 Development: theme 1

7:54 Theme 1 in relative minor

8:25 Più mosso: theme 2A

8:49 Theme 2B: (violin solo)

9:29 Recapitulation: theme 2A

9:53 Recapitulation: theme 2B (violin solo)

10:11 Recapitulation: theme 2A

10:20 Molto ritardo: cello solo; transition to recapitulation of theme 1

10:34 Recapitulation: theme 1 (cello and violin duet)

12:05 Allegro: closing section: uses themes from III

12:54 V (VII): coda: allegro vivo: theme 1A*

*Section VI was eliminated from this performance of the work

13:25 Theme 1B

13:55 Closing

DISC 2

Act III
No. 14: Moderato*

*This scene was eliminated from this performance of the work

Track 4:

No. 18: Scene (Allegro)

0:00 Theme 1

0:29 Development

0:49 Recapitulation: theme 1

0:59 Allegro giusto

1:13 Allegro giusto (continued): recapitulation of andante from finale Act I and opening Act II

Track 5:

No. 19: Pas de six

0:00 I (II): intrada/moderato assai: theme 1*

*"Moderato assai" is labeled "II" in notes but in score is the subheading of the intrada

0:50 Theme 2

1:05 Transition back to theme 1

1:33 Recapitulation: theme 1 with development

2:24 Recapitulation: theme 2 with closing

2:46 III: variation I: allegro: theme 1

3:05 Theme 2

3:40 Recapitulation: theme 1 with development

4:19 IV: variation II: andante con moto: theme 1

4:46 Development 1

5:08 Development 2

5:30 Recapitulation: development 1

5:52 Theme 2

6:19 Development

7:17 Coda

8:06 V: variation III: moderato: theme 1

8:23 Development

8:31 Transition

8:35 Recapitulation: theme 1

8:45 VI: variation IV: allegro: theme 1

8:59 Development 1

9:12 Development 2

9:25 Recapitulation: theme 1 with closing

9:40 VII: variation V: moderato: harp solo

10:01 Allegro simplice: theme 1

10:21 Development

10:40 Recapitulation: theme 1

10:54 Più mosso to closing

11:11 VIII: coda: allegro molto vivace: theme 1

11:38 Coda: cadence

11:44 Theme 2

11:57 Transition back to theme 1
with development

12:31 Closing

Numéro supplementaire: Pas de deux

0:00 I: introduction: moderato

0:36 II: andante (violin solo):
theme 1A

1:14 Theme 1B

1:48 Theme 2A

2:05 Theme 2B

2:36 Transition with clarinet solo

3:04 Theme 3 (tutti)

4:15 III: variation I: allegro
moderato: theme 1A

4:31 Theme 1B

4:43 Transition back to theme 1A

4:47 Recapitulation: Theme 1A
(tutti)

5:05 IV: variation II: allegro:
theme 1

5:20 Theme 2

5:34 Recapitulation: theme 1

5:49 V: coda: allegro molto vivace:
theme 1

6:14 Theme 2

6:39 Recapitulation: theme 1

6:51 Theme 3

7:16 Recapitulation: theme 1

7:29 Theme 4

7:52 Recapitulation: theme 1 with
closing

No. 20: Danse hongroise: Czardas

0:00 Moderato assai: introduction

0:15 Allegro moderato: theme 1

0:53 Development

1:19 Recapitulation: theme 1

1:46 Coda to allegro; transition to
vivace

1:55 Vivace: theme 1

2:17 Development: theme 1 in
minor; transition to
recapitulation

2:29 Recapitulation: theme 1 with
coda

7 *Serenade for Strings, in C, Opus 48,* with short works including *Barber: Adagio for Strings.* Simeon Bychkov conducting the Berlin Philharmonic Orchestra. Philips 434 108-2.

Tchaikovsky's adoration of the music of Mozart showed up in several of his mature works: the *Rococo Variations* for cello and orchestra, the last of his four *Orchestral Suites* (subtitled *Mozartiana*) and the *Serenade for Strings.* That graceful work takes off from some of Mozart's early *Divertimentos,* but maintains one foot in Tchaikovsky's own time, as its waltz clearly demonstrates. The robust, intense lyrical style of Tchaikovsky did not die with his passing, of course; in Samuel Barber's popular *Adagio* (originally a movement from his *String Quartet No. 1,* now expanded for full string orchestra) it lives again.

TRACKS 1-4:

Serenade for Strings

Track 1:

Pezzo in forma di sonatina

- **0:00** Introductory theme
- **0:31** Theme in lower strings
- **0:59** Variation on introductory theme
- **2:13** First theme
- **2:42** First theme: development
- **3:08** First theme: return
- **3:43** Second theme
- **4:15** First theme: fragment
- **4:33** Second theme: return
- **5:28** First theme: return
- **5:52** First theme: development
- **6:23** First theme: return
- **6:59** Second theme: return
- **7:30** First theme: fragment
- **7:49** Second theme: return
- **8:44** Introductory theme: return

Track 2:

Waltz. Moderato (Tempo di valse)

0:00 First theme

0:58 First theme: embellished

1:18 Second theme

1:58 First theme: return

2:56 First theme: embellished

3:35 First theme: fragments

Track 3:

Élégie. Larghetto elegiaco

0:00 First theme

0:31 First theme: repeat, with variations

1:27 Second theme

1:59 Second theme: variation I

2:36 Variation II

2:58 Variation III

3:49 Variation IV

4:14 Variation V

4:47 Transition

5:18 Cadenza passage (violins)

5:40 First theme: return

6:15 First theme: variation

7:34 Second theme: new variation

8:14 Coda

8:38 First theme: fragment

Track 4:

Finale: Andante/allegro con spirito

0:00 Introductory theme

0:37 Introductory theme: development

1:36 First theme ("tema russo")

1:55 First theme: variation

2:09 Second theme

2:29 Second theme: variation

3:19 First theme: development

4:13 First theme: variation

5:08 Second theme: return

5:27 Second theme: variation

6:26 Third theme: introductory theme from track 1

6:49 Third theme: variation

7:02 First theme: final return

Track 5:

Italian Serenade in G (Hugo Wolf)

0:00 Introduction

0:09 First theme

0:46 Second theme

1:04 First theme: fragment

1:19 Third theme

1:47 Transition

2:00 Fourth theme

2:49 First theme: variation

3:27 Second theme: return

4:26 Fifth theme

4:53 Fifth theme: fragment

5:04 Fifth theme: development

5:59 Transition

6:28 First theme: return

7:28 Introduction: variation

TRACKS 6-7:

Introduction and Allegro (Edward Elgar)

Track 6:
Introduction

0:00 First theme, part I

0:27 First theme, part II

1:15 Second theme: solo viola

1:43 Solo violin entrance

2:50 First theme, part I: return

3:25 Second theme: return

Track 7:
Allegro

0:00 Second theme from introduction (track 6): development

1:00 Third theme

1:43 First theme from introduction (track 6), part I: return

2:19 Transition

2:32 Third theme: partial return

2:41 First theme: partial return

2:55 Second theme: partial return

3:24 Fugue

4:03 Fourth theme

5:32 Third theme: partial return

5:50 Second theme: return

6:41 Third theme: return

7:15 Transition

7:25 First theme, part I: return and development

8:00 Transition

8:14 Third theme: partial return

8:27 Second theme

9:35 First theme, part II: return

Track 8:
Adagio for Strings (Samuel Barber)

0:00 First theme

0:24 Second theme

0:51 First theme (with extension)

1:49 Second theme

2:09 Second theme (with extension)

8 Arias from *Eugene Onegin, The Queen of Spades, The Sorceress, Yolanta and Mazeppa* (with arias from five operas by Giuseppe Verdi). Dmitri Hvorostovsky, baritone, with Valéry Gergiev conducting the Rotterdam Philharmonic Orchestra. Philips 426 740-2.

Of all the Tchaikovsky operas, *Eugene Onegin* remains the most popular, in Russia and around the world. Tchaikovsky's music mirrors the sad desperation of Pushkin's Tatyana and the dashing but shallow Onegin who insults her and lives in regret. The young Siberian baritone with the unpronounceable name offers an interesting survey across Tchaikovsky's operatic style; each of his chosen arias deals with love—unrequited here, rewarded there. The contrast between the declamatory Russian arias and the creamy lyricism in a selection of arias from Verdi operas is striking, as are the similarities; Tchaikovsky himself held Verdi's music in high regard.

Track 1:

Yevgeni Onegin: Vy mne pisali

0:00 Orchestral introduction

0:24 Voice enters: accompagnata recitative

1:31 Orchestral interlude: change of mood

2:04 Aria begins: first verse (B flat major)

2:40 Second verse

3:11 Middle section (verse 3):

relative minor (G minor)

3:55 Return to B flat major

4:35 Coda

Track 2:

Yevgeni Onegin: Uzhel' ta samaja Tat'jana

0:00 Orchestral introduction: clarinet and strings (C sharp minor)

0:26 Voice enters: recitativo accompagnato

1:09 Aria begins (B flat major)

1:29 Second verse

1:52 Finale: orchestral coda

Pikovaya Dama: Vy tak pichal'ny, daragaya

0:00 Orchestral introduction: English horn solo

0:14 Voice enters: accompanied recitative; various orchestra solos

1:08 Aria begins (E flat major)

1:47 Second verse (repeat of music in first verse)

2:00 Musical extension of second verse; development

3:00 Recapitulation of first verse with orchestral variation

3:36 Second verse (music of first verse) with variations

3:49 Musical extension of second verse

4:26 Coda verse

4:48 Variation of coda verse

Verdi: La Traviata: Di Provenza il mar

0:00 Orchestral introduction: wind solos (C sharp major)

0:24 Aria begins: voice, first theme

1:55 Interlude: repeat of introductory material

2:18 Second verse: same music as verse 1, new text

3:49 Coda begins

3:58 Cadenza

4:25 Final cadence

Macbeth: Perfidi!... Pieta, rispetto

0:00 Orchestral introduction: tutti, forte

0:27 Voice enters: accompanied recitative

1:18 Calmer character to close recitative

1:49 Aria begins (D flat major)

2:16 Second verse: begins with same music as verse 1

2:50 Arrival at dominant key: middle section in minor mode

3:17 Modulation to E major

3:36 Sudden modulation back to D flat major

3:54 Recapitulation of first verse: violin melody, voice descant

4:13 Voice with orchestra in unison

4:36 Coda begins

4:45 Cadenza

5:10 Final cadence

Track 6:
Luisa Miller: Sacra la scelta

0:00 Orchestral introduction (D flat major)

0:09 Voice enters: first verse

0:27 Second verse: same music as first verse

0:46 Middle section

1:06 Transition back to tonic key

1:12 Cadenza

1:21 New material in return to tonic key

1:43 New material repeated

2:05 Coda to first verse

2:16 Cadenza

2:32 Final cadence, first verse

2:41 New orchestral material for second stanza

2:48 New vocal material in A flat major

3:22 Repeat of new vocal material, extended

3:43 Orchestral interlude; false cadence (C major)

3:54 Restatement of new vocal material in A flat major

4:10 Harmonic transition: D flat major to E flat major

4:28 Restatement of new vocal material

4:49 Coda begins

5:13 Final orchestral cadence

Track 7:
Charodeika: Dela, pravlenija

0:00 Orchestral introduction for strings (unison) (C sharp major)

0:21 Voice enters: accompanied recitative, alternating with unison strings

1:44 Orchestral climax leading to arioso

1:59 Arioso begins over dominant pedal tone in G major

2:27 Agitated middle section; highly chromatic and dramatic

2:57 Return to gentle arioso in G major

3:19 Dramatic material returns over tremolo strings

3:37 Return to arioso tonality

4:10 Coda-like material begins over tonic pizzicato pedal

4:36 Harp text painting

4:42 Final cadence

Iolanthe: Kto mozhet

0:00 Furious orchestral introduction

0:08 Voice enters, tempo of introduction (E major)

0:24 Brief modulation to C major

0:37 Return to E major

0:43 Aria, part II; modulatory development, middle section

1:07 Return to E major

1:21 More modulatory development

1:39 Return to orchestral introduction

1:45 Recapitulation of first vocal entrance

2:02 Brief modulation to C major

2:18 Return to E major

2:24 Short coda

Mazeppa: O, Marija, Marija!

0:00 Orchestral introduction: clarinet, cello solos

1:03 Voice enters; free accompagnato (F sharp major)

2:03 Cello solo

2:11 Restatement of first vocal theme

2:21 Restatement of clarinet solo

2:31 Second theme, faster

2:55 Restatement of principle vocal theme

3:04 Modulation to B flat major

3:17 Middle section; chromatic development

4:06 More agitated development

4:50 Return to tonic key (F sharp major); coda-like material

5:19 Final vocal statement

Verdi: Il Trovatore: Tutto e deserto

0:00 Pizzicato string introduction (F major)

0:25 Voice enters: accompanied recitative with strings

1:24 Transition material

1:31 Aria begins with orchestral triplet accompaniment

1:40 Voice enters with first theme (B flat major)

2:27 Modulatory middle section

2:59 Return to first theme with ornamentation (B flat major)

3:23 New material in B flat major

3:50 New material repeated

4:16 Cadenza

4:47 Final cadence

Don Carlos: Son io, mio Carlo

0:00 Slow string introduction (C major)

0:38 Oboe solo over tremolo strings

0:57 Restatement of string introduction

1:25 Voice enters; accompanied recitative (strings)

2:20 Aria begins: voice, first theme (E flat major)

2:42 Restatement of first theme, modulating to dominant

3:05 Orchestral interlude, harmonic development

3:15 Voice imitates interlude theme; modulation

3:46 Return to tonic key; variations on first theme

4:09 Brief modulatory development

4:35 Return to tonic key over dominant pedal point

4:54 Tonic pedal point

5:05 Interlude; funeral march (trumpets) (C sharp minor)

5:24 Voice commentary over trumpet march

5:40 Middle section of march: dominant (G sharp major)

6:12 Lyrical new vocal melody (C sharp major)

6:55 Sudden restatement of heroic theme from early in opera (A major)

7:24 Recapitulation with variations of lyrical C sharp major melody

8:05 Sudden cadence on agitated diminished chord

8:14 Cadenza

8:26 Rousing final statement by orchestra

9 *String Quartet in D, Opus 11 (*with *Borodin: String Quartet No. 2 in D).* Played by the Emerson String Quartet. Deutsche Grammophon 427 618-2.

Both quartets have at least this in common: their respective slow movements lent their melodies to American popular songs. Tchaikovsky's became "The Isle of May"; Borodin's turned into "Baubles, Bangles, and Beads," in the musical *Kismet,* whose score was entirely derived from his tunes. These are slight works compared to their respective composers' orchestral and operatic outputs, but they are at least proficiently fashioned; their place in the chamber music repertory is deservedly secure.

TRACKS 1-4:

String Quartet No. 1 in D

Track 1:
Moderato e semplice

- **0:00** Theme 1
- **0:53** Theme 1 with short development
- **1:30** Theme 2
- **1:47** Theme 2 with short development
- **2:22** Poco più mosso (closing theme)
- **2:55** Development: themes 1 and 2
- **4:33** Recapitulation: theme 1

- **5:15** Recapitulation: theme 1 with short development
- **5:49** Recapitulation: theme 2
- **6:39** Poco più mosso: closing theme
- **6:59** Allegro (closing)

Track 2:
Andante cantabile

- **0:00** Theme 1, part I
- **0:38** Theme 1, part II
- **1:20** Recapitulation: theme 1, part I
- **2:07** Theme 2
- **3:27** Recapitulation: theme 1, part I with development
- **4:53** Recapitulation: theme 2 with

different accompaniment

6:03 Closing section

Track 3:

Scherzo

0:00 Allegro ma non tanto: theme 1

0:20 Theme 2

0:45 Recapitulation: theme 1

1:04 Repeat: theme 2; recapitulation: theme 1

1:49 Trio, part I

2:01 Trio, part II

2:15 Recapitulation: trio, part I

2:26 Recapitulation: trio, part II

2:38 Da capo: repeat theme 1, theme 2, recapitulation theme 1; end

Track 4:

Finale

0:00 Allegro giusto: introduction to theme 1

0:14 Theme 1

0:32 Theme 1 with development

1:05 Introducion to theme 2

1:16 Theme 2

1:36 Transition back to theme 1 (used as closing section)

2:07 Development: derived from themes 1 and 2

3:25 Recapitulation: theme 1

3:48 Recapitulation: theme 2

4:19 Recapitulation: theme 1

4:51 Development

5:20 Andante: transition to closing section

5:41 Allegro vivace: closing section

TRACKS 5–8:

String Quartet No. 2 in D (Aleksandr Borodin)

Track 5:

Allegro moderato

0:00 Theme 1

1:00 Closing theme; transition to theme 2

1:15 Theme 2

2:19 Closing theme/transition/ritard

2:43 Allegro moderato: recapitulation and development

4:45 Recapitulation: theme 1

5:45 Further development and use of first closing section

6:02 Recapitulation: theme 2 with development

Glossary

Arpeggio The word comes from *arpa* (Italian for "harp"); it denotes a succession of notes, at least three, that outline a **harmony.** If played simultaneously, they are a chord. Composers who wanted to define the **tonality** of a work at the outset often devised melodies that began by outlining the basic harmony of that tonality: for example, the famous first *Prelude* in Bach's *Well-Tempered Clavier,* which is nothing but an arpeggiated sequence of harmonies. The clangorous chords that begin Tchaikovsky's *First Piano Concerto* form an arpeggio that spells out the harmony of the grand opening theme.

Chamber music A self-explanatory concept: music meant to be played in close-in surroundings, in a style that is intimate and subtle. Chamber music uses only a single instrument on a part, as opposed to orchestral music where several violins, violas, or cellos may be playing in unison. The sovereign chamber-music form, from the eighteenth century to the present, is the string quartet (two violins, viola, and cello); Tchaikovsky composed three. The piano trio (piano, violin, and cello) was also a popular chamber-music medium. Tchaikovsky's single work in that genre was composed as a memorial for Nikolay Rubinstein.

147

Chromatic In the most familiar harmonic system, the musical octave (from C, say, to C) is divided into twelve half-steps, known as chromatic steps. The diatonic musical scale, which is the basis of a piece in a given tonality—C major, for instance—is a pattern of seven tones from those possible twelve, an arrangement of half- and whole-steps. Any other notes—an F-sharp, say, in the key of C—are dissonances, the alien resources a composer uses to enrich his music, the friction that makes the wheels turn. The history of music in the nineteenth century is, as much as anything, the history of composers expanding the vocabulary of dissonance and thus blurring the sense of tonality. It's anybody's guess, for long stretches in the first movement of Tchaikovsky's *Fifth Symphony,* or the battle music in *Romeo and Juliet* as to what is the actual tonality at any given moment, and that uncertainty becomes part of the drama. Don't confuse dissonance with discord, which is a valueless value-judgment word.

Classical At its purest, the term refers to the ancient world. The Classical revival in the eighteenth century used ancient models (such as the Parthenon) to define its passion for clear, logical structures in all the arts, and so the term is used to describe the works of this time. Tchaikovsky's music is full of his high regard for bygone musical styles: the *Rococo Variations for Cello,* and his *Fourth Orchestral Suite* subtitled *Mozartiana.* Used more loosely, "Classical" also refers to music meant to be heard against a background of silence by audiences trained (perhaps intimidated?) to applaud only at the end—as opposed to "pop." We also use the term for anything that has been around for a while: the Tchaikovsky *Fifth Symphony,* the Rolling Stones, the original Coca-Cola recipe, Jaguars (the car, not the animal).

Concerto *Certare* means "to battle" or "struggle"; *con* means "with". The concerto pits small forces against large ones: soloist and orchestra locked in wordless struggle. Mozart ennobled the form, turning his concertos into heartfelt "conversations" rather than mere show-off pieces. Tchaikovsky's best-known concertos, one for piano and one for violin, were hated by the critics at the time but loved by whatever virtuosos could master their difficulties.

Counterpoint or **polyphony**   Many lines of music going on simultaneously create a contrapuntal (or polyphonic) texture. In opera, the device allows for a stageful of characters, each expressing a different thought but all woven together. The depth in much of Tchaikovsky's music—in the developments of the first and fourth movements of the *Fifth*, or the climactic battle music in *Romeo and Juliet*—stems from his mastery of counterpoint as a dramatic device.

Form   In the broadest sense, musical form (or structure) is the composer's way of involving a listener's memory in the unfolding of a piece. One reacts to the initial music, follows a pathway to contrasting ideas, is stirred when the material returns or when the composer subjects it to new variations. The great composers are the ones who are most successful in finding ways to stretch the meaning of form to allow for individual expression. By Tchaikovsky's time, the strict outlines of the classical forms that had served Mozart and Beethoven quite well had begun to blur. But we can still feel their pull in the way the opening themes in all four movements of the *Fifth Symphony* return several times in the movement (with contrasting material interspersed). The first and last movements, in particular, follow the **sonata form** outline, with the principal thematic material presented in contrasting tonalities in the exposition, swirled around some in the development, returned intact in the recapitulation, and give way to a grand summing-up in the coda.

Harmony   This refers to the ability to hear more than one tone at a time, to react to the way these simultaneous tones blend into a consonance or dissonance, and to follow the way one harmony will lead to the next to produce a progression. Dissonant harmonies set up an expectation; consonant harmonies resolve it into a feeling of arrival, and this process continues, over and over, sweeping the music to its stable, logical fulfillment.

Melody The horizontal aspect of music (as harmony is the vertical), the rising-falling line of expression that results from connecting the dots. Early music was nothing *but* melody, given a relationship to time (long notes versus short notes) by its rhythm. Other civilizations have built elaborate musical systems solely on melody; listen, for example, to the wonderful complexity of Indian classical music as played by Ravi Shankar—it is pure melody.

Movement This is a section of a longer work (concerto, symphony, sonata) which is musically complete in itself. In works of several movements, the composer usually arranges them to provide contrast: fast followed by slow, complex followed by simple. In Beethoven's time, audiences saw nothing wrong with separating the movements of one work with other composers' music and, therefore, applauded at the end of each movement.

Nineteenth-century composers began to see multi-movement works as single expressions. Tchaikovsky's *Fifth Symphony,* unified by the reappearance of the Fate motive in every movement, is an example of the integrated symphony. Some audiences today are still ensconced in the eighteenth century, however, and spoil the continuity by clapping between movements.

Opera The emergence of opera is usually dated at the start of the seventeenth century, when several Italian composers sought to "reform" music by reviving the Greek ideal of sung drama. Two centuries later, Italy remained the prime proving ground, where singers reigned supreme and sensible plots were secondary. Other countries—Germany, France, and Russia in particular—found ways of injecting their national spirit into operas; Russian composers especially turned many of their works into grand nationalistic pageants, demanding great virtuosity from singers and set designers. The best of Tchaikovsky's operas, however, used deeply romantic, tragic texts by the country's poet/hero, Aleksandr Pushkin: the bitter irony of *Eugene Onegin*, the supernatural manifestations in *The Queen of Spades*.

Romantic The Romantics believed in the inseparable marriage of the arts and the human soul. They cultivated modes of expression that stirred the emotions and inflamed the imagination, producing goosebumps through the creation of painful beauty. By the same token, the musical Romantics worked hard to blur the outlines that had well served the Classical era: the distinction between keys and between structural elements so that, for example, exposition flowed into development without a break, and that the first theme of Tchaikovsky's *Fifth Symphony* didn't merely define the key of E-minor; it also defined Fate.

Sonata It simply means "sounded" or "played" (as opposed to *cantata*, which means "sung"). In Romantic usage the sonata was a piece for one instrument (keyboard) or two (violin and piano), in several movements. Symphonies, concertos,

string quartets: these are members of the sonata family as well, distinguished only by the performing forces they demand.

Sonata form This could just as easily be called "symphonic" form; it refers to the wonderfully logical and flexible organization of materials within an instrumental movement, practiced by composers in the Classical era and respected (if only in its non-observance) by composers of later times. The essence of the sonata form is contrast: between a first theme and melodies introduced later, between one tonality and another, between a slow rate of tonality change and a fast one, between material when first heard and the subtle changes it undergoes later. With all those variables, sonata form became a great dramatic battlefield on which composers from Beethoven to Tchaikovsky could exercise with exquisite and awesome freedom. After Tchaikovsky's time, the sonata form began to drift out of favor, largely because the new chromatic harmonic language made the contrast between keys difficult to hear and subsequently irrelevant.

Tonality (or **key**)   From the Renaissance until early in the twentieth century, it was a given that Western music followed a system of tonality defined by the succession of harmonies derived from the notes of a given scale (see **chromatic**). The tonic of the key (the note C, for example, in the key of C) served as the point of origin, departure, and ultimate return; the music began in its given tonality, strayed somewhere else, and then returned, sometimes quite dramatically. The destiny of music, after the clear horizons of classicism, seems like an ongoing attempt to blur the sense of tonality. The cloudy opening of Beethoven's *Ninth Symphony* is certainly a further step in that direction, much imitated by later composers. In our own century, the innovative composer and theorist Arnold Schoenberg declared the integrity of non-tonal (i.e., atonal) music, while also proclaiming that there was still plenty of good music waiting to be written in the key of C.

Tone poem (also **symphonic poem**) The Romantics believed that even music without a text should be *about* something—a story, a hero, a philosophic concept, all clearly described by the tone-color and overall mood of the music. Tchaikovsky called his *Romeo and Juliet* an "overture-fantasy," but it's really a tone poem in which themes clearly relate to the characters in Shakespeare's tragedy; the form of the music, therefore, is dictated by the sequence of events in the play: the battles among rival street gangs in Verona, the dialogue between the lovers, the final tragedy in which the couple's theme takes on a sad new harmonic coloration.

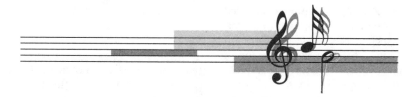

Further Reading and Listening

General Histories

Calvocoressi, M.D. and Gerald Abraham. *Masters of Russian Music.* London: Duckworth, 1936.

Lang, Paul Henry. *Music in Western Civilization.* New York: W.W. Norton, 1941.

Schonberg, Harold. *Lives of the Great Composers.* New York: W.W. Norton, 1981.

Swafford, Jan. *The Vintage Guide to Classical Music.* New York: Vintage, 1992.

Writings on Tchaikovsky

Abraham, Gerald, ed. *The Music of Tchaikovsky.* New York: W.W. Norton, 1974.

Brown, David. "Tchaikovsky" in *The New Grove Dictionary of Music and Musicians.* London and New York: Macmillan, 1980.

Poznansky, Alexander. *Tchaikovsky, The Quest for the Inner Man.* New York: G. Schirmer, 1991.

———. "Tchaikovsky's Death: Myth and Reality" in *Nineteenth-Century Music,* Vol. 11, p. 199. Davis, CA: University of California Press, 1988.

Tchaikovsky, Modest (translated by Rosa Newmarch). *Life and Letters of Tchaikovsky.* London 1906, reprinted New York: Harmony House, 1973.

Weinstock, Herbert. *Tchaikovsky.* New York: W.W. Norton, 1943.

A Selective Tchaikovsky Discography

Manfred. Mariss Jansons conducting the Oslo Philharmonic Orchestra. Chandos 8535.

Piano Concerto No. 2 (with Prokofiev: *Piano Concerto No. 1*). Michael Boriskin, pianist, with Michael Bartos conducting the Polish National Radio Symphony. Newport Classic NPD 85520.

Fatum (with *Capriccio Italien* and the *Symphony No. 4*). Evgeni Svetlanov conducting the USSR Symphony. Melodiya SUCD-10-00196.

Piano Sonata (with excerpts from *The Months*). Barry Douglas, pianist. RCA 7887-2-RC.

The Sleeping Beauty (complete): Leonard Slatkin conducting the
St. Louis Symphony. RCA 09026-61682-Z.

The Tempest (with ***Hamlet*** and other works). James DePreist
conducting the Oregon Symphony. Delos DCD 3081.

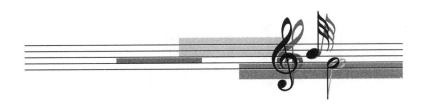